TOP 201
CONSPIRACY THEORY
VIDEOS
on
YOUTUBE

LUCAS L. JACKSON

Printed in the United States of America

First Printing, 2017

ISBN-13: 978-1981444359
ISBN-10: 1981444351

Lucas L. Jackson
lucasljackson@gmail.com

Creative Design Consultants
Benjamin L. Jackson
Lola K. Jackson

About Top 201
Conspiracy Theory Videos on YouTube

Television has changed a lot over the years. It wasn't so long ago that many people could only get one or two channels on their television set and they had to use aluminum foil as rabbit ears on their antennas to achieve that!

Then in the 80s we were introduced to cable and everyone wanted their MTV. Suddenly our options for television consumption were increased by an enormous amount and with a clarity and sharpness that we had never before thought possible.

After the introduction of cable, things didn't change much for decades. New channels were introduced that focused on a narrower and narrower viewing audience. This increased the total number of channels available but created a highly fragmented cable universe.

In the mid-90s the internet came along but we really didn't start watching videos and streaming television shows until sometime in the mid-00s. And then along came YouTube and everything changed. Suddenly, we had a way to get around the pre-programmed world of cable and watch videos online.

We started to realize that we could watch any show, any movie, any television commercial or any other video we've ever seen, anytime we wanted! This new ability, when combined with fast internet speeds, made YouTube and platforms like it the cable television of the future.

YouTube offers everyone - from big production companies to individuals on their smart phones - a platform for releasing content about absolutely anything they want. This has allowed people to further specialize the content they want to see by creating it themselves.

About Top 201
Conspiracy Theory Videos on YouTube
continued...

One particular genre that has thrived on YouTube has been the realm of conspiracy theories. Conspiracy theories are interesting for many reasons but the one element they all share in common is that they question some mainstream narrative that's been presented as truth or fact.

The purpose of this book is to provide the reader with a list of engaging, interesting, thought-provoking videos to watch with friends, loved ones or in thoughtful contemplation alone.

The author is not advocating or recommending any particular view, theory, statement or presentation. The author encourages everyone to listen to arguments made point-by-point and determine if they make logical sense or not.

The author also does not advocate or recommend any particular channel, group or individual. The author has not met and does not know any of the individuals associated with any of the videos featured in this book. Some of the channels I feature are very popular with conspiracy theorists, some are quite reviled and still others are both. Make up your own mind after watching some of their content.

It is the mark of an educated mind to be able to entertain a thought without accepting it.

-Aristotle

I hope you enjoy watching these videos as much I enjoyed preparing this book.

Lucas L. Jackson

TOP 201 CONSPIRACY THEORY VIDEOS ON YOUTUBE

911 Fakery

TOP 201 CONSPIRACY THEORY VIDEOS ON YOUTUBE

911 Fakery

15 years of deception; 9/11 reviewed

Channel: WeAreChangeRotterdam

https://www.youtube.com/watch?v=_JwxzVlLLwQ

Description: On 11 September 2001, the world was shocked. It proved to be a milestone in history. Suddenly we were "at war"; a 'war on terror' we were told that proved to be endless and hopeless. Fifteen years after the event, this 'WeAreChange.NL' documentary challenges your ability "to see what you see" and invites you to critically re-examine and take responsibility accordingly regarding the impact of 9/11 on our lives.

TOP 201 CONSPIRACY THEORY VIDEOS ON YOUTUBE

911 Fakery

9/11 - What Happened to the Passengers?

Channel: NRUN65

https://www.youtube.com/watch?v=mGB9A4ODmFo&t=33s

Description: 9/11 revisited - This video examines evidence of the impossibility, because of the technology in use in 2001, of the airborne cell phone calls from the nine passengers that were indicated on the Caller-ID's of the recipients as recorded in FBI reports. The technology for such calls did not exist in 2001.

TOP 201 CONSPIRACY THEORY VIDEOS ON YOUTUBE

911 Fakery

9/11 Trillions: Follow The Money

Channel: corbettreport

https://www.youtube.com/watch?v=n3xgjxJwedA

Description: Forget for one moment everything you've been told about September 11, 2001. 9/11 was a crime. And as with any crime, there is one overriding imperative that detectives must follow to identify the perpetrators: follow the money. This is an investigation of the 9/11 money trail.

911 Fakery

6

9/11 - AN INCONVENIENT 9/11 TRUTH [Part I] (2017 version)

Channel: Truther TV

https://www.youtube.com/watch?v=BJkl0GJu0Yc

Description: This was initially reinterpretation of Ryan Dawson's versions of 'War By Deception', by DJ Thermal Detonator spliced along with 'Core Of Corruption: In The Shadows' and the Mike Rivero portions of 'Fabled Enemies' and other worthy portions from popular truth documentaries like '9/11: Mysteries', 'Zietgiest', "Who killed John O'Neill?', 'Zero: 9/11', 'Ring Of Power', 'Welcome To Terrorland: 9/11, Mohamed Atta and the Venice Flying Circus' and others…

911 Fakery

Christopher Bollyn: The Man Who Solved 9/11

Channel: Know More News

https://www.youtube.com/watch?v=pLWIV0TTcbI

Description: Investigative journalist, 9/11 researcher, and author Christopher Bollyn sits down with Adam Green and Know More News for an exclusive interview.

We discuss: His Books and Tour, Israeli Role in 9/11, Predictive Programming, Alex Jones controlled opposition, and much more!

911 Fakery

Conclusive Evidence the 9/11 Planes were NOT REAL

Channel: 911PlanesHoax

https://www.youtube.com/watch?v=CUoqwUVOxHE

Description: Incontrovertible - New 9/11 documentary by Tony Rooke
A film for Coppers & Fire Fighters by Coppers & Fire Fighters.
Buy the standard definition DVD or Blu-ray version of the film from
http://www.incontrovertible911evidenc...

911 Fakery

Incontrovertible - New 9/11 Documentary by Tony Rooke

Channel: 911familymember

https://www.youtube.com/watch?v=y5UyynjxAyw

Description: Incontrovertible - New 9/11 documentary by Tony Rooke
A film for Coppers & Fire Fighters by Coppers & Fire Fighters.
Buy the standard definition DVD or Blu-ray version of the film from
http://www.incontrovertible911evidenc...

911 Fakery

No Planes on 911 - Part 1 by Gari Jones

Channel: checktheevidence

https://www.youtube.com/watch?v=9teNgS3oC4E

Description: This is a slightly edited version of a compilation video made by Gari Jones. You can see the full video here: https://vimeo.com/115801417
Here is Gari's description: This video is dedicated to everyone who still believes that real planes crashed on 9/11. I ask everyone to forget everything you have learned or have been told about 9/11. Start here with a fresh clean slate and let your mind go blank.

911 Fakery

September 11 - The New Pearl Harbor (Full version) - Part 1 of 3

Channel: NRUN65

https://www.youtube.com/watch?v=I5ppQDmId9M

Description: 9/11 Revisited - Road to 9/11 - The world we live in today is largely a direct result of the events of September 11, 2001. This 3-part documentary is an extremely detailed examination of what really happened on the day that changed the course of the world.

911 Fakery

Stand for the Truth: A Government Researcher Speaks Out | 9/11 Evidence and NIST

Channel: ae911truth

https://www.youtube.com/watch?v=GvAv-114bwM

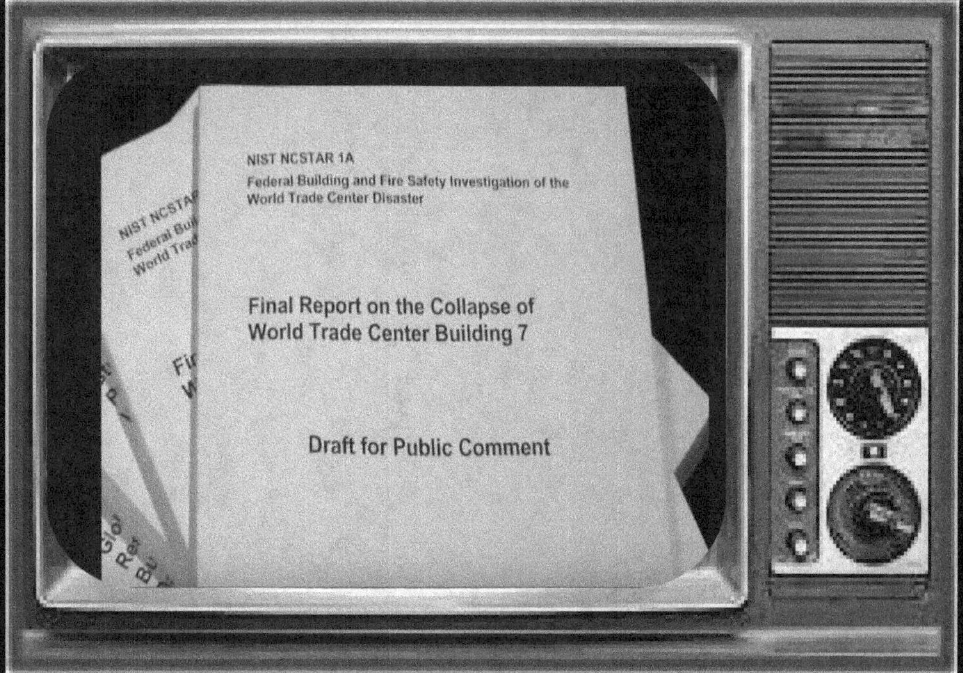

Description: In August 2016, Peter Michael Ketcham, a former employee of the National Institute of Standards and Technology (NIST), began looking into the reports his agency had released years earlier on the collapse of the World Trade Center. What he found shook him to the core.

911 Fakery

The Eddie Bravo Conspiracy Compilation –
The Joe Rogan Experience

Channel: JRE Clips

https://www.youtube.com/watch?v=csFBzzTyGeA

Description: Isolated from Best of the Fight Companion VOL. 2

911 Fakery

14

Trump On 9/11: "Bombs Must Have Been Used "

Channel: ron johnson

https://www.youtube.com/watch?v=poY5BQ49gf0

Description: On Sept. 11, 2001, Donald Trump called a New York TV slot to share what he had seen from his high rise condo and what he had gotten notification from partners nearer to the World Trade Center. At a certain point amid the almost 10-minute meeting, Trump specified that his working in the Financial District was presently the tallest.

Chemtrails
&
Geoengineering

Chemtrails & Geoengineering

Chemtrails | 100% Proof | Geoengineering

Channel: ODD Reality

https://www.youtube.com/watch?v=Hd2jA0lT8N0

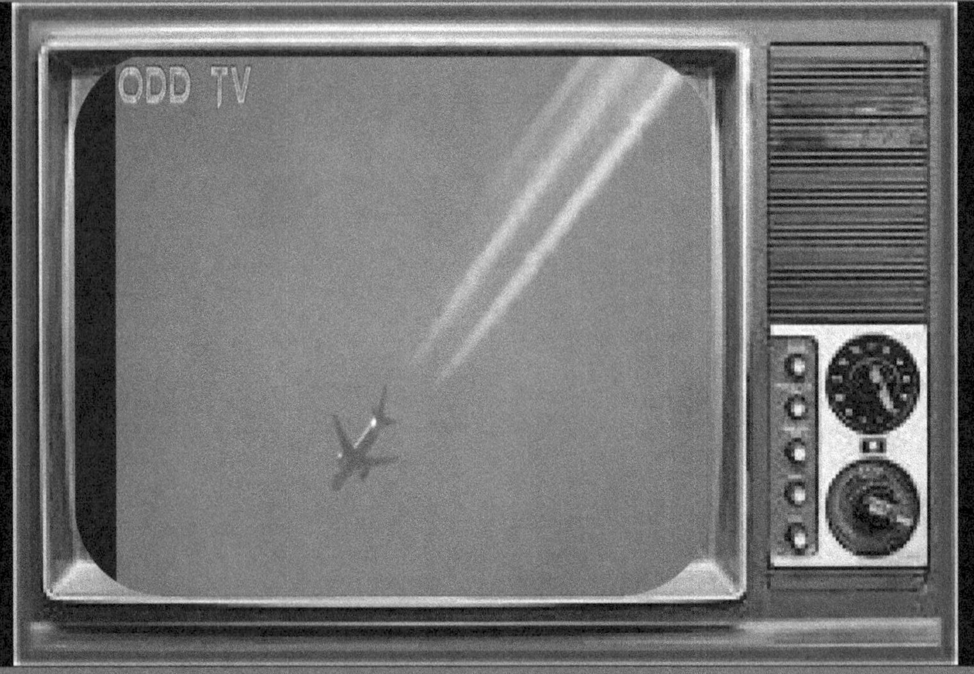

Description: The term "chemtrails" was transformed into a derogatory term long ago. If you mention the word, you're considered insane and paranoid. The proper term is geoengineering and Solar Radiation Management (SRM). One component of this secret geo-engineering program is known as chemtrails.

Chemtrails & Geoengineering

Elana Freeland - Chemtrails, HAARP, and the Full Spectrum Dominance of Planet Earth

Channel: Veritas Radio

https://www.youtube.com/watch?v=IisMqiJRbQk

Description: This interview examines how chemtrails and ionospheric heaters like the High-frequency Active Auroral Research Project (HAARP) in Alaska service a full-spectrum dominance.

Chemtrails & Geoengineering

HAARP Caught on RADAR 2017

Channel: Captain Nowledge

https://www.youtube.com/watch?v=S0vdnSDhRg8

Description: Engineering Storms HAARP 2017 .. Blizzard of '78

Chemtrails & Geoengineering

How To Protect Agaist Effects of Chemtrails and Fluoride

Channel: Unchained Brain

https://www.youtube.com/watch?v=bkGyx47xvPs

Description: Helpful suggestions to detox from fluoride and aluminum
Music by Chris Zabriskie
Before commenting about Trump, watch "I Was Wrong about Trump.".

Chemtrails & Geoengineering

NASA Satellite Images Prove Storms Can Be Man Made - Cloud Seeding & HAARP

Channel: #SeekingTheTruth

https://www.youtube.com/watch?v=GRW1yOMIgsA

Description: Evidence has emerged from NASA that the recent outburst of extreme hurricanes in the U.S. are as a result of man-made weather manipulation. Patrick Roddie, a geoengineering expert, discovered newly released NASA Worldview satellite images that show weird anomalies around hurricanes Harvey and Irma, and the paths they are about to follow.

Chemtrails & Geoengineering

THE CHEMTRAILS GIRLS - STOP GEOENGINEERING NOW - DOCUMENTARY

Channel: ChemTrailsMN

https://www.youtube.com/watch?v=plMt2e15WFw

Description: THE CHEMTRAILS GIRLS STOP GEOENGINEERING NOW MINI DOCUMENTARY share this!

Chemtrails & Geoengineering

ChemTrails in Cali - #WEDONOTCONSENT

Channel: Harvey Dent's Return

https://www.youtube.com/watch?v=p7BFg4RpsRQ

Description: #WeDoNotConsent Get the f*ck outta here with that sh*t

AUTHOR'S NOTE: I tried to show a video posted by Crrow777 on chemtrails but Crrow777's channel was deleted by YouTube before I published.

TOP 201 CONSPIRACY THEORY VIDEOS ON YOUTUBE

Chemtrails & Geoengineering

WATCH QUICKLY BEFORE They DELETE This VIDEO!

Channel: CreepyTV

https://www.youtube.com/watch?v=J-vd_nOCnsA\

Description: WATCH QUICKLY BEFORE They DELETE This VIDEO!

Dinosaur Hoax

TOP 201 CONSPIRACY THEORY VIDEOS ON YOUTUBE

Dinosaur Hoax

ARE DINOSAURS REAL?

Channel: TruthUnveiled777

https://www.youtube.com/watch?v=fp_LS6vi_V0

Description: THE TRUTH REVEALED!!!!!!! For many centuries, we have been taught and spoon-fed the lies that animals and humans have "evolved," that dinosaurs are millions and millions of years old, and that dinosaurs were wiped out by a so-called "comet" some-odd tens-of-millions of years ago. But Is This TRUE?

TOP 201 CONSPIRACY THEORY VIDEOS ON YOUTUBE

Dinosaur Hoax

Dinosaurs Debunked in 3 minutes!

Channel: Truth Seekers Channel

https://www.youtube.com/watch?v=CmGXRIN7TTo

Description: The Dinosaurs were a hoax. In this video I debunk the existence of the dinosaurus in 3 minutes. Dinosaurs are fake, they did not exist! I am not giving Dinosaurs fact here, but just a logical explanation of the dinosaurus hoax! Dinosaur extinction is a false theory and dinosaur fossils are also fake artefacts.

Dinosaur Hoax

Dinosaurs Never Existed!

Channel: Eric Dubay

https://www.youtube.com/watch?v=5KXzgeq1BuA

Description: The following video was taken from "The Flat Earth Conspiracy" book by Eric Dubay:
http://www.lulu.com/spotlight/ericdubay

Dinosaur Hoax

**The DINOSAUR Conspiracy - LOST Episode - SPACE ERASED
The NASA FRAUDCAST - FLAT EARTH - EP 116**

Channel: Nasa Fraudcast Channel

https://www.youtube.com/watch?v=eza8fL1oX9g

Description: Chris dives into the theory that Dinosaurs and their history may be an entirely made-up hoax. Discussion also includes the Great Bone Wars and the deceitful nature of many, if not most, major historical museums around the United States.

Dinosaur Hoax

The Dinosaur Hoax is an Absurd Fallacy

Channel: Insanity is Sanity

https://www.youtube.com/watch?v=Z8Hbxexn7Qc

Description: No one has to date put forward an argument that is acceptable in favour of the Dinosaur myth. All they have are insults.

The Dinosaur theory is based on lies and fantasy.

Evolution Hoax

Evolution Hoax

Big Bang Evolution is a Masonic Lie Hiding Intelligent Design

Channel: Eric Dubay

https://www.youtube.com/watch?v=JkEL4yBJxm8

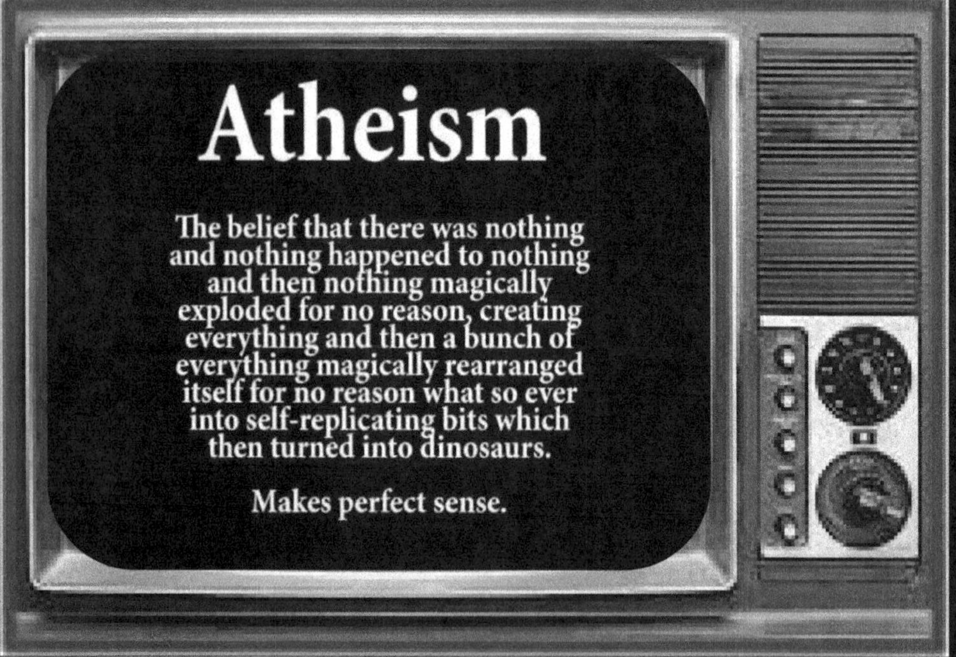

Description: In the following presentation taken from my book, "The Flat Earth Conspiracy," I present the case for intelligent design and expose the many scientific frauds and Masonic connections of Darwinism and its main proponents throughout history. You will see how Neanderthal Man, Piltdown Man, Nebraska Man, Peking Man, Orce Man, Turkana Boy, Lucy and all other supposed ape-man transitional species were fakes and fabrications made by Masonic...

Evolution Hoax

Evolution Is Scientifically Impossible

Channel: Shill Stoppers

https://www.youtube.com/watch?v=bqdnGP8gf3k

Description: Darwinism Is A SCAM Just Another Elite LIE

Evolution Hoax

Evolution The Greatest Lie EVER Told !!!
Evolution Debunked by White Rabbit of The CTN

Channel: The Vigilant Christian

https://www.youtube.com/watch?v=QV9zTOTxQNs

Description: Evolution is the greatest lie ever told to humanity! So many blindly believe this lie because they have been brainwashed to believe it is scientific fact! When in reality science proves it to be wrong! In this video I share with you an awesome video from CTN team member white rabbit who debunks this supposed fact! Please share this video! God Bless and STAY VIGILANT !!!

Evolution Hoax

Evolution Theory MODERN MYTH // Ancient Man was NOT primitive

Channel: GlobalObserveR

https://www.youtube.com/watch?v=86WZBzP9cHo

Description: Main purpose of this video is not to prove or dismiss any "theories" but rather to present some authentic pieces of ancient masonry along with intriguing artifacts pointing to the simple fact that we are NOT "first and only" advanced civilization on this planet. There were much more advanced cultures before us that were wiped out either by great cataclysm or nuclear war type scenario.

Evolution Hoax

Lawrence Krauss Scientism's Cult Leader Lies About Evolution

Channel: jeranism

https://www.youtube.com/watch?v=Do5l1Vvzl5E&t=1261s

Description: This video contains several important points but for the most part, it points out the lies that Lawrence Krauss is willing to tell to push his cult's needed dogma of evolution. Pay close attention to the blatant lies and remember that when telling the truth, there is no need to lie in every other sentence.

Flat Earth

Flat Earth

5 Potential Answers to "Why would they Lie?"
(A Flat Earth Discussion)

Channel: D. Marble

https://www.youtube.com/watch?v=OR5UXx9BpEA

Description: In this video I outline a list of reasons as to why "they" would lie to us about the shape of the Earth and the true nature of reality itself.
Spread the Truth, Expose the Lies, Demand Answers! #FEOffensive

Flat Earth

9 Lunar Waves Filmed - Game Change

Channel: Crrow777

https://www.youtube.com/watch?v=0mi0w8bLtUM&t=181s

Description: This clip includes the 9 lunar or moon waves (hologram?) filmed to date. Four are from other videographers and five from me. There is no longer any debate as to the reality of the lunar wave as an actual real event that has been taking place on our moon for some time. Crrow777 podcast website: https://www.crrow777radio.com

Flat Earth

ACTUAL FOOTAGE OF THE STARS AND PLANETS | "WANDERING STARS" as Captured by Curious Truth Seekers.

Channel: All Seeing Heart

https://www.youtube.com/watch?v=tNHU5KOI9lQ&t=508s

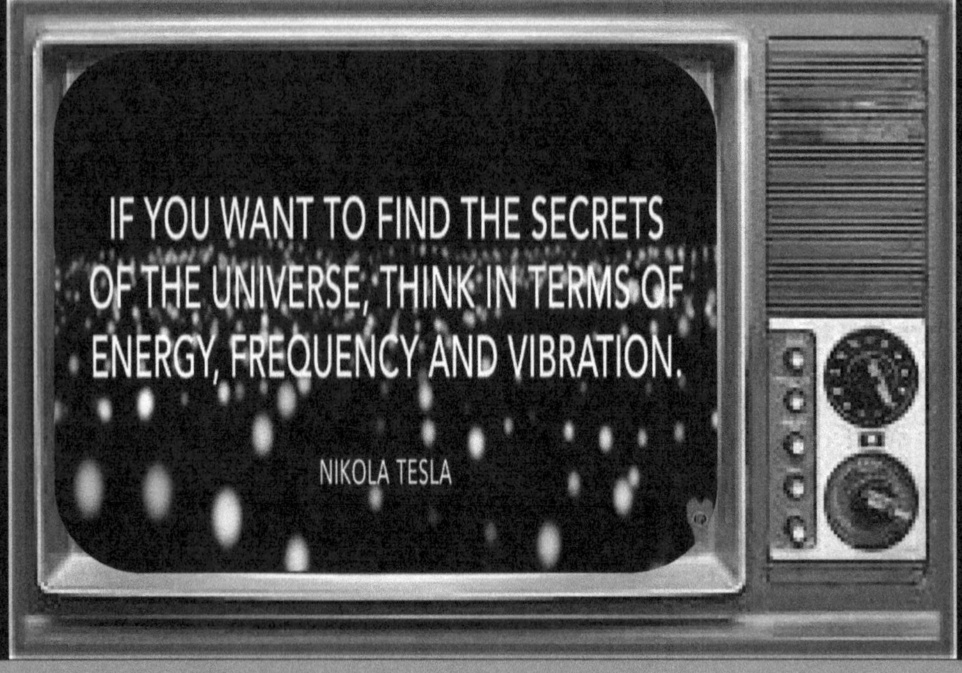

Description: "Actual footage of the stars and planets (wandering stars) above our heads each night. This video is of actual footage of stars mixed with Cymatics, Sonoluminescence, Bioluminescence, Harmonic Resonance of water, Light, the electromagnetic firmament and the waters above."

Flat Earth

Bill Nye vs Flat Earth Asshole

Channel: Flat Earth Asshole

https://www.youtube.com/watch?v=1f-x3Hj3lQU

Description: This heavyweight matchup started innocently enough with me watching Bill Nye "The Science Guy" when I was a young child. Fast forward nearly three decades later and here we are doing battle by way of intellectual discussion and debate over the true shape of the earth. Can the man, the myth, the legend which is Bill Nye "The Science Guy" prove the earth is a sphere and defeat Jake Gibson "The Flat Earth Asshole Guy

Flat Earth

Bravo, Gracie, Dubay, Flat Earth Conspiracy

Channel: Eric Dubay

https://www.youtube.com/watch?v=aoLSgtC_y6w

Description: I have remastered this recent ground-breaking podcast, cleared up almost all of the audio issues, removed irrelevant chit-chat, and added relevant pictures, maps, diagrams and videos turning this into a jam-packed 3-hour presentation of the world's biggest deception, the mother of all conspiracies, the Flat Earth. Please share this with the sleepy sheeple in your life and help spread the good news: Earth is flat, and that's a fact, now let's shake off these parasites once and for all.

TOP 201 CONSPIRACY THEORY VIDEOS ON YOUTUBE

Flat Earth

FLAT EARTH - ALMIGHTY GRAVITY

Channel: odiupicku

https://www.youtube.com/watch?v=XgvypHZX9wo

Description: Special thanks to my dear friend DON QUIXOTE whose two videos i have borrowed while i was making this video !
Thanks also goes to DITRH, and to some other guys whose videos i have used (as well), taking out from them some clips which i found suitable for setting up this compilation...

Flat Earth

Flat Earth - If You Tolerate This...

Channel: Antonio Subirats

https://www.youtube.com/watch?v=qMkdHcaRwkw

Description: Jordan Peterson's Channel -
https://www.youtube.com/user/JordanPe...

Please watch and listen - https://youtu.be/cX8szNPgrEs

Flat Earth

Flat Earth - Taking to the streets of Edinburgh

Channel: Beyond the imaginary curve

https://www.youtube.com/watch?v=p5asOJGkCQI

Description: Thanks again to john smith and the lovely people of edinburgh, get out and talk to your fellow man, they don't bite :)

Flat Earth

Flat Earth - The Rest of the Story

Channel: Komorusan714

https://www.youtube.com/watch?v=Tr1-WRrhgtg&t=1510s

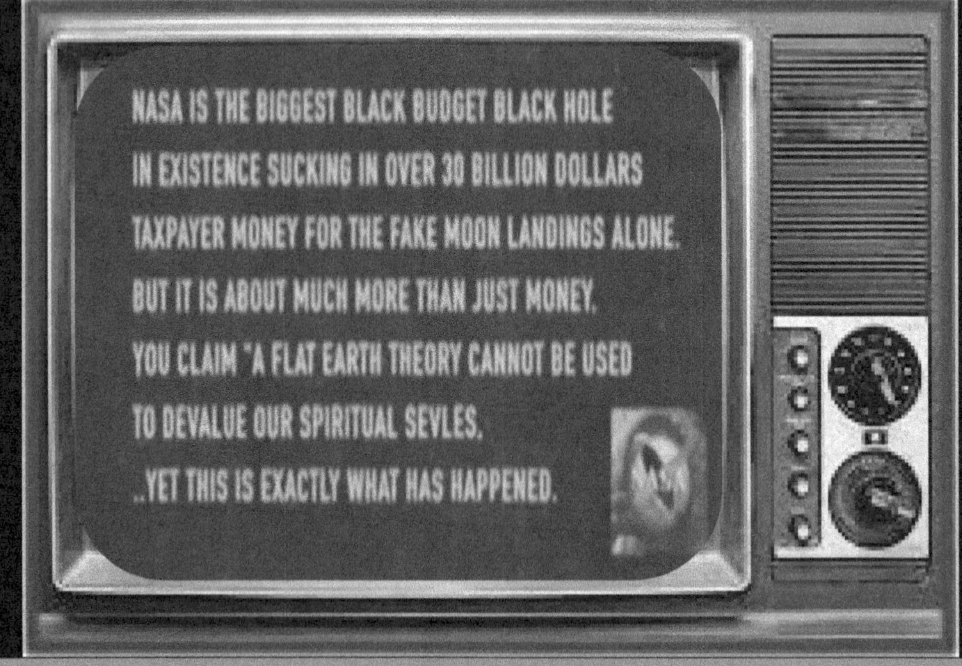

Description: The Age of Deception is over

Flat Earth

Flat Earth - The Truth, The Mockery & The Proof!

Channel: Flat Earth Hub

https://www.youtube.com/watch?v=TcbOet-QYUM

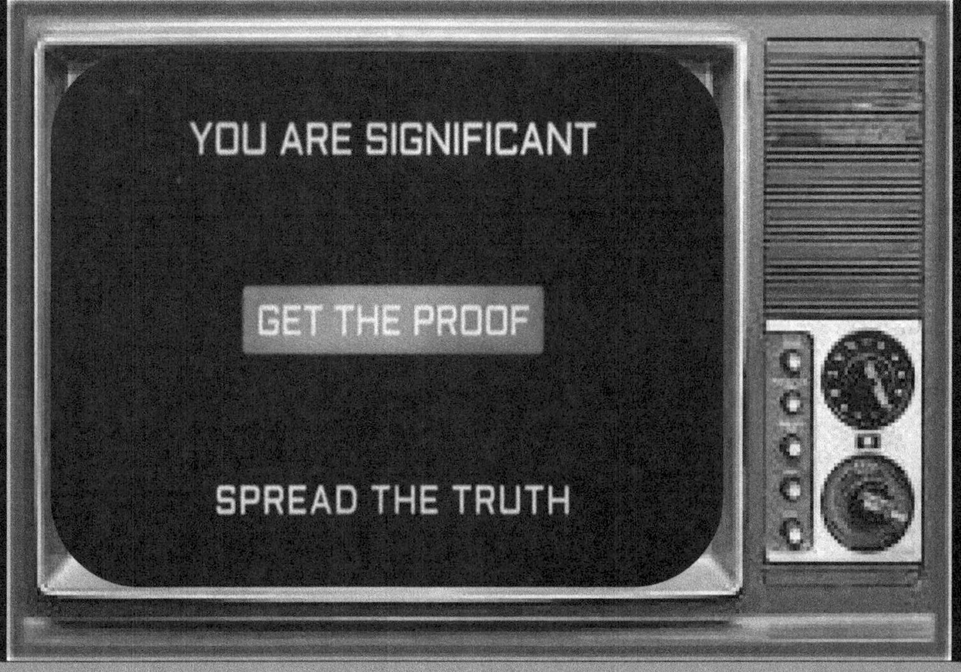

Description: The Principle : A must watch : Spread the Truth!

Our Simple Question : Where is the Curve?

Flat Earth

FLAT EARTH - The WATERS ABOVE - Outside the DOME there is WATER ...

Channel: Adam 1414

https://www.youtube.com/watch?v=FUFvtVdYkqI

Description: FLAT EARTH - The Waters ABOVE - Outside the DOME there is WATER ... is SPACE filled with Water? Water ... Water Everywhere .... Do we Live Underwater? The biblical passages say clearly that the waters of the Great Flood came also from the "Windows of Heaven" .... the windows of heaven were opened and shut up to allow the waters above to enter the flat earth ...

Flat Earth

FLAT EARTH | 4 Hour Documentary by Russianvids (RV TRUTH)

Channel: theTRUman

https://www.youtube.com/watch?v=I5ZN289jjDo&t=3272s

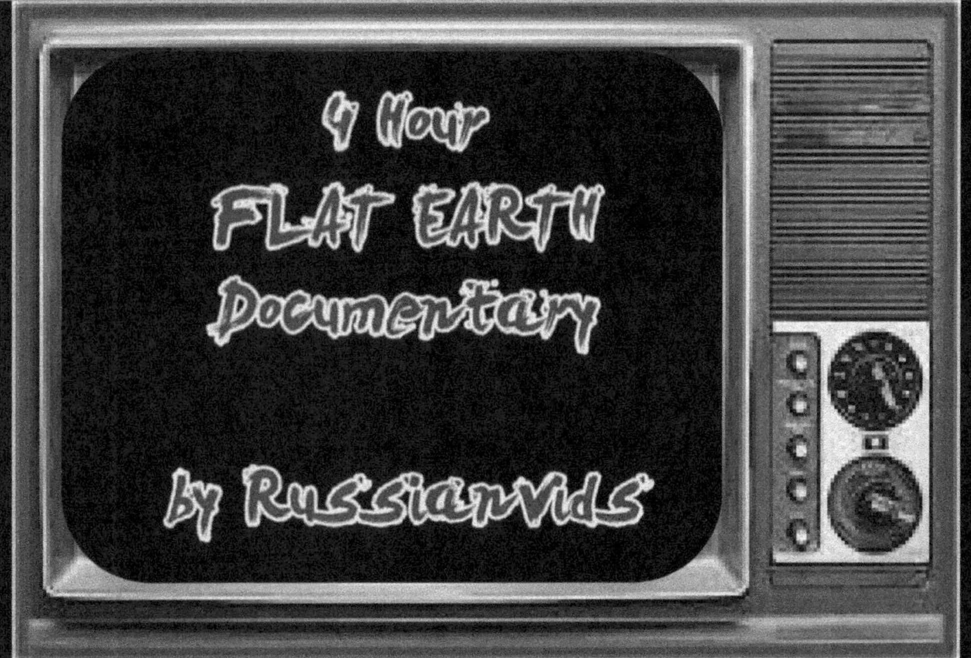

Description: My first attempt at uploading this was a failure. It was *blocked WORLDWIDE* over a 90second clip from a movie that was released in the 1980's. Seriously YouTube and Warner Bro's? You two can suck each others @#$% and go to $#@! Anyways....so, what'd I do? I loaded it into my movie editor and removed the 90second clip and reuploaded all 4 hours. Take that Warner Bro's and YT, you @#$%'s. *CLAIMING FAIR USE* originally uploaded by the channel "Russianvids"

Flat Earth

Flat Earth | Joe Rogan & Neil deGrasse Tyson Gets Destroyed In 16 Minutes

Channel: You Been Exposed

https://www.youtube.com/watch?v=rVUkuI7ST7Q

Description: FLAT EARTH - The Waters ABOVE - Outside the DOME there is WATER ... is SPACE filled with Water? Water ... Water Everywhere ....

Do we Live Underwater? The biblical passages say clearly that the waters of the Great Flood came also from the "Windows of Heaven" .... the windows of heaven were opened and shut up to allow the waters above to enter the flat earth ...

Flat Earth

FLAT EARTH Clues Introduction - Mark Sargent

Channel: markksargent

https://www.youtube.com/watch?v=T8-YdgU-CF4

Description: Are we inside a Truman show enclosed world, thousands of miles wide? This is part of a series of videos that shows not only is it possible, but likely. The Flat Earth awakening is the biggest story to hit this world in Millennia. I am humble to be just a part of this massive force of truth, one that's going to change the world and how you live forever.

Flat Earth

Flat Earth Physics: Episode 4.0 –
The ISS, satellites, and the thermosphere

Channel: Flat Earth Talk

https://www.youtube.com/watch?v=QwXKzyHTiKw

Description: Brian Mullin's "Balls Out Physics" series: Episode 4.0 - "The ISS, satellites, and the thermosphere" His physics series prove the earth is not a globe. This proof the earth is flat, or at least not a spinning ball, by an engineer Brian Mullin. His channel is no longer available so I cannot post a link there. I don't know what happened to Brian and why his channel is gone. If you do, please let us know in the comment section of this video. Thanks for watching Flat Earth Talk

Flat Earth

Flat Earth, Mt. Meru And The Lost Book Of The North: The Full Inventio Fortunatae

Channel: FlatWater FlatEarth

https://www.youtube.com/watch?v=zidKgyfUB40&t=1499s

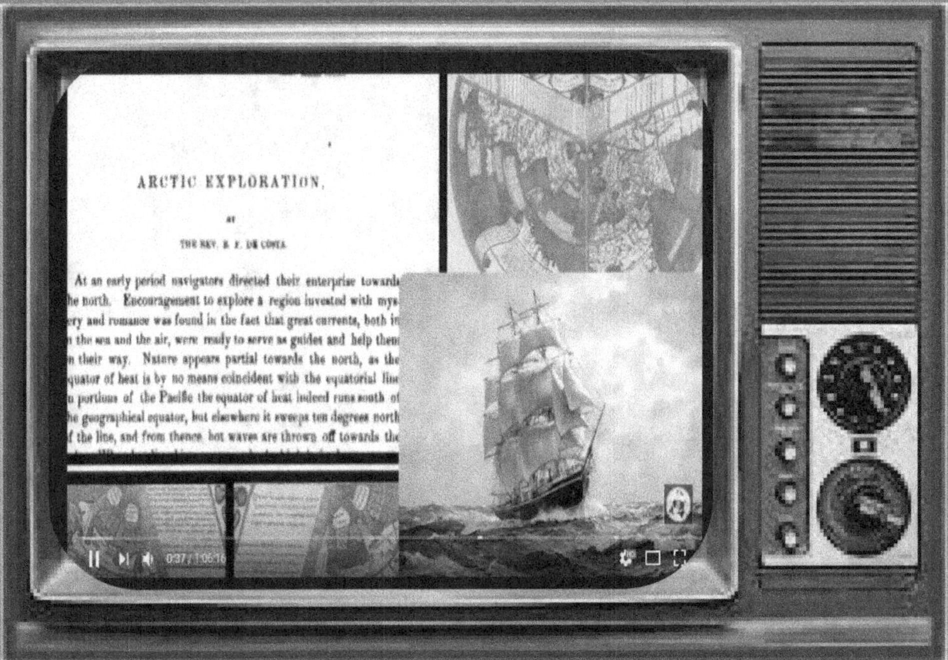

Description: In this film I read the Inventio Fortunatae, (The Fortunate Discovery), a pretty old, rare document, hidden from public view, full of the first reports from northern explorers. These ancient reports are more likely to describe the real physical attributes of Earth at the North Pole.

Flat Earth

From JFK, Apollo, 9/11 To Flat Earth: How TV Fakes Images, Fools the World & Creates a False Reality

Channel: Flat Earth Truth

https://www.youtube.com/watch?v=HTA_0nyAlwo

Description: Television - the weapon of mass media to commit mass deception by The Powers That Be to dupe the world into believing falsehoods such as three of the greatest conspiracies uncovered in modern times - the JFK Assassination, the Apollo moon missions, and 9/11. These epic hoaxes were passed off as real news stories to make people believe in lies such as that a lone gunman killed JFK, that man went to the moon several times (without mishap at that) in the 60s...

Flat Earth

How Flat Earthers become Flat Earthers – DITRH, ODD TV and more

Channel: Al Theeathoone

https://www.youtube.com/watch?v=FlcOi7xqqNg

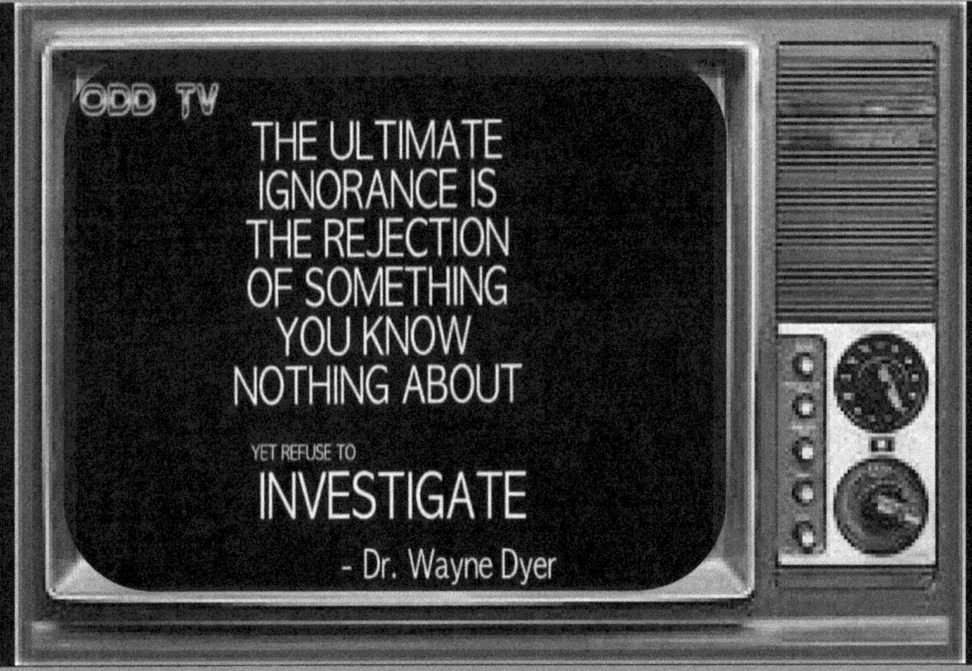

Description: Flat Earthers reveal how they became and remain Flat Earthers

Flat Earth

IMPOSSIBALL 🌎 Flat Earth Documentary (2017)

Channel: Celebrate Truth

https://www.youtube.com/watch?v=UbYtkrTquXE

Description: Get ready for the IMPOSSIBALL! A surprise flat earth documentary from Robbie Davidson of Celebrate Truth (John 14:6)

Flat earth proof of the biggest conspiracy theory documentary film!

Flat Earth

Kevin James Knows The Earth Is Flat!! #FlatEarth

Channel: Rv Truth Over Tradition

https://www.youtube.com/watch?v=srhtivBBb6I

Description: NO COPYRIGHT INFRINGEMENT - Credit to whoever owns it for the video clips. The use of these clips is not to undermine the copyright that whoever owns it has on this fight but to educate and engage the audience in what really transpired during the event. Thank you.

TOP 201 CONSPIRACY THEORY VIDEOS ON YOUTUBE

Flat Earth

**MUST SEE!!! No satellites in space!
Just balloons above the Flat Earth**

Channel: Peter Pan

https://www.youtube.com/watch?v=PxXGcc5OdmA&t=2425s

Description: No satellites in space! Just balloons above the Flat Earth

Thanks to PLANATE VERITAS for the original video.

Flat Earth

ODD TV's Flat Earth Trilogy

Channel: ODD Reality

https://www.youtube.com/watch?v=ARp2j8t3O8Q

Description: This is a compilation of my first 3 flat earth videos from late 2015 and early 2016. They make for a good and solid 2 hour flat earth documentary that's packed with great information. This video has been made and uploaded due to multiple requests by my subscribers and my friends. Thanks for all your support.

Flat Earth

Proof the Moon is Not 238900 miles away

Channel: RichieFromBoston

https://www.youtube.com/watch?v=3rzt6U08gzM

Description: Watch in its enirety before you comment, these are too hard to understand. They are spraying us like a bug. And its exactly why Alzheimer's Autism ADD are at epidemic proportions. RFB

Flat Earth

Rocket hitting the flat earth dome

Channel: GeoShifter

https://www.youtube.com/watch?v=IAcp3BFBYw4

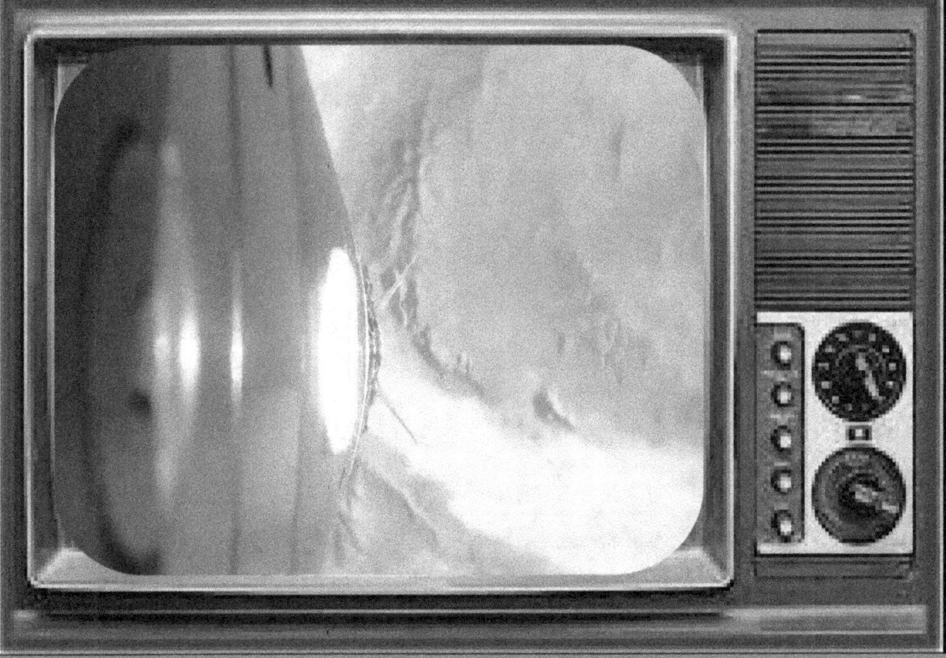

Description: Follow up video:
https://www.youtube.com/watch?v=L4eY_N9IS3w

Flat Earth

The History of Flat Earth

Channel: Eric Dubay

https://www.youtube.com/watch?v=pGl8I3l-5ac&t=906s

Description: International Flat Earth Research Society President Eric Dubay presents the complete history of Flat Earth from the beginning of recorded history to today. Please help share this most important presentation with as many as you can. Also please be sure to download and re-upload this and my other videos so they cannot censor us all. Thanks so much to all my subscribers.

Historical Myths

Historical Myths

#noenginesmatter Pearl Harbor was a hoax:
Current Affairs series

Channel: Awake Souls

https://www.youtube.com/watch?v=yvZ7EFZkebE

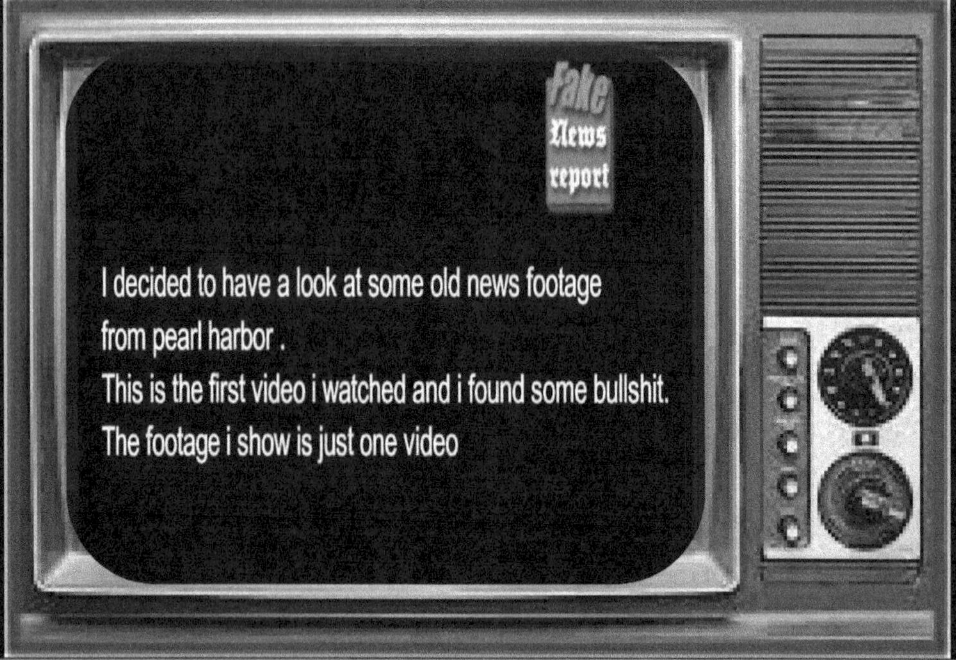

Description: Copyright Disclaimer Under Section 107 of the Copyright
Act 1976: Allowance is made for fair use for purposes such as criticism,
comment, news reporting, teaching, scholarship, and research. Fair use
is a use permitted by copyright statute that might otherwise be
infringing. Non-profit, educational or personal use tips the balance in
favor of fair use. This work contains original work of commentary and
critical analysis. Quotations are attributed to the original authors...

TOP 201 CONSPIRACY THEORY VIDEOS ON YOUTUBE

Historical Myths

ARCHAEOLOGICAL COVER UP

Channel: WISE UP

https://www.youtube.com/watch?v=PvvIHbSIjAo

Description: Destruction Of Ancient Sites

Historical Myths

Everything you've been taught about ancient history is a lie PT.1 Link to part 2 in description

Channel: Hubcap _

https://www.youtube.com/watch?v=us-7d1x_9RM

Description: As in the days of Noah.....global high tech society....and presence of the "Fallen ones". These structures were built in the antideluvian period. The whole Idea that these were built by the Egyptians is a lie....more like a joke! These structures were there and the Pharaoh decided to use it as a tomb! There are many attempts to recreate these structures by the ancient Egyptians and you can see their mini , crumbling , mud pile attempt.

Historical Myths

FLAT EARTH | The Giza Pyramids & Sphinx HOAX (2-part series)(MUST SEE!)

Channel: theTRUman

https://www.youtube.com/watch?v=aslJhR-o1Sw&t=131s

Description: originally uploaded by the channel "Dave Johnson" titled "The Giza Plateau pyramids are a HOAX built mid 1700 into 1800's few hundred years old. (part 1)" & ""Pyramids" of Giza & the Sphinx HOAX built mid 1700 into 1800's few hundred years old. (part 2)"

TOP 201 CONSPIRACY THEORY VIDEOS ON YOUTUBE

Historical Myths

History is A lie Agreed Upon

Channel: WISE UP

https://www.youtube.com/watch?v=5N-0M4WDhog

Description: Forgot to mention mountains in my description of the Antediluvian or PREdiluvian world. . . . -ie- . The pillers -- soil -- AND mountains.

Historical Myths

kingdrop 2017 | No Pyramids on Flat Earth! Excavated or Constructed?? | Coosa "Little Egypt" pt 1

Channel: 432 The Drop Radio

https://www.youtube.com/watch?v=oj7ePlK_Vjc

Description: Please subscribe for the latest drop. Our goal is to raise the frequency of our indigenous community by promoting "Vibration Awareness" and discussing our most relevant topics and solutions.

Historical Myths

Pearl Harbor.. Another False Flag

Channel: AltInvestorshangout

https://www.youtube.com/watch?v=brFagWVQ0kM

Description: Pearl Harbor.. Another False Flag

Historical Myths

Proof the Grand Canyon monuments are ancient pyramids

Channel: Lee Bracker

https://www.youtube.com/watch?v=CgOa2eccPVk

Description: There is a reason why the Monuments of the Grand Canyon are named for Egyptian Pharaohs, but not because Egyptians were present on this continent. David Hatcher Childress (first voice) erroneously and without correction delivers history from a 1909 article that never mentions Egypt or Egyptological principles as part of the experience within the Grand Canyon subterranean expedition.

Historical Myths

Pyramids of Giza & the Sphinx HOAX built mid 1700 into 1800's few hundred years old part 2

Channel: Zero11s

https://www.youtube.com/watch?v=PpXzEDJKa8o

Description: Original by Dave Johnson

Historical Myths

Santa Claus the Magic Mushroom

Channel: Eric Dubay

https://www.youtube.com/watch?v=TX2Zkzt0KMU&t=1s

Description: Have you ever wondered why on Christmas we cut down/carry evergreen trees inside our houses, decorate them with fancy ornaments, and place presents underneath them? Under this tree is where those who are deemed good find their reward in the form of a present. A big red and white rounded mushroom grows under the very tree we are to look under on Christmas morning to find our gift

Historical Myths

Stonehenge Hoax Exposed

Channel: Providence

https://www.youtube.com/watch?v=24jsbVl3RFY

Description: Stonehenge is fake. Exposed.

Historical Myths

Stonehenge is FAKE! No Longer Authentic. Reassembled With Cranes.

Channel: jeranism

https://www.youtube.com/watch?v=OjmY5zak28o

Description: I used to think Stonehenge was cool and mysterious. Now it is as cool and mysterious as gum on my shoe. My video shows that Stonehenge is clearly not an ancient site. Was it once? Who cares? But now it has been taken down and rebuilt a few times just in the last 100 years. So, it is AT BEST a replica. Of course it is still in school books and on National Geographic with no mention of all the concrete filler and cranes used to erect the former ancient site.

Historical Myths

The "Negro/Black" civilization of ancient America

Channel: All Eyes On Media

https://www.youtube.com/watch?v=anWOGIGOiik

Description: "The first South Americans ... exhibited an undisputed morphological affinity firstly with Africans and secondly with South Pacific populations."   "...the earliest South Americans tend to be more similar to present Australians, Melanesians, and Sub-Saharan Africans (narrow and long neurocrania; prognatic, low faces; and relatively low and broad orbits and noses)."

Historical Myths

Untold Truth About Dr. Martin Luther King Jr. – All Involved w/ His Assassination Came Out Publicly!

Channel: Dane Calloway

https://www.youtube.com/watch?v=EiWv6dgUS8A

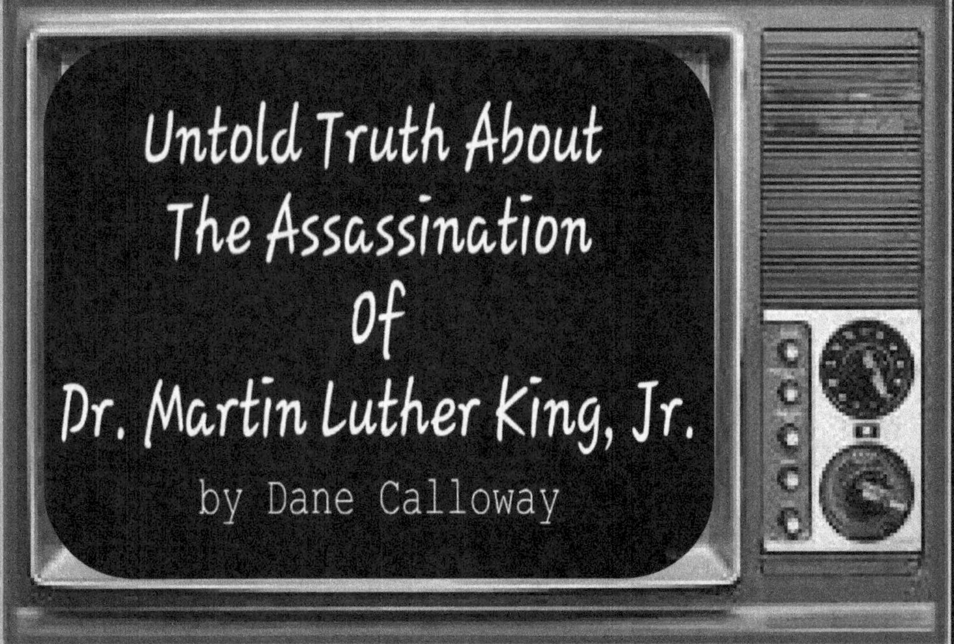

Description: ALL NEW VISITORS CAN SUBSCRIBE TO MY CHANNEL HERE
-
(Thumbs up this video!) http://youtube.com/c/DaneCalloway
HELP SUPPORT MY CHANNEL & CONTENT HERE - (Contribute to keep
this ship sailing & earn rewards!) http://patreon.com/danecalloway

NASA Fakery

NASA Fakery

A Funny Thing Happened on the Way to the Moon

Channel: Bart Sibrel

https://www.youtube.com/watch?v=xciCJfbTvE4

Description: Award winning filmmaker Bart Sibrel (Sibrel.com) presents his highly acclaimed (and much hated) controversial documentary showcasing newly discovered behind-the-scenes out-takes from the first mission to the moon, proving conclusively that the crew never left earth orbit.

NASA Fakery

**All of Nasa's lies and nonsense
boil down to this disturbing video**

Channel: Captain Obvious

https://www.youtube.com/watch?v=pCICm2v0Nt8

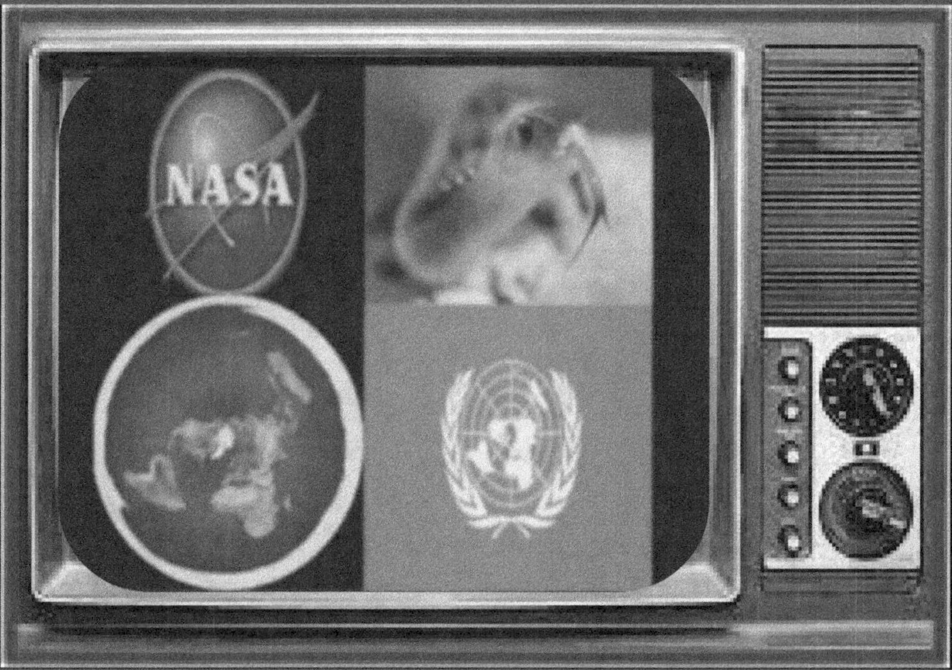

Description: What you're about to see and witness will prove beyond a shadow of a doubt that Nasa is a complete CGI Occult institution by Captain Obvious.

NASA Fakery

BBC Documentary The moon landing hoax

Channel: dp8

https://www.youtube.com/watch?v=VsvQDCXWICo

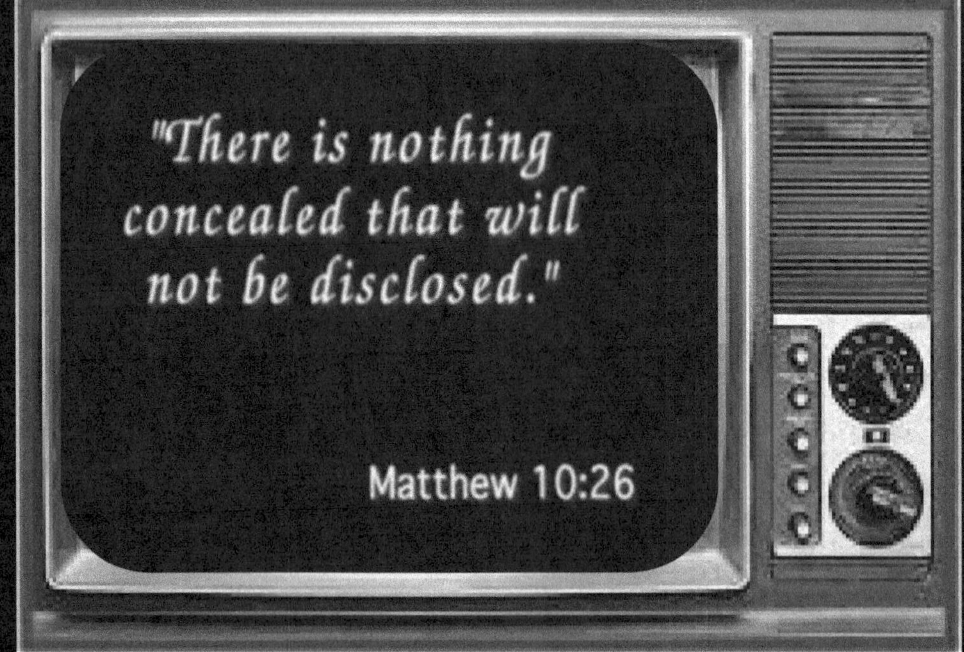

Description: No comment

NASA Fakery

Compilation Of Space Hoax and NASA LIES Videos Great Flat Earth vs Globe Video

Channel: Hank Cooper

https://www.youtube.com/watch?v=bkaznZoQwfs&t=140s

Description: Credit to Flat Earth Asshole as I think most if not all comes from his work, check other videos on this channel for more. Published on Dec 22, 2016 This is a compilation of video clips which provide excellent evidence that all outer space travel is entirely fictional. Rockets do not go to outer space, man has never walked on the moon, nothing has ever landed on Mars, and the ISS is a complete hoax as well!

NASA Fakery

Dave Murphy on Late Night With Milenko / Bro Sanchez "Why It's Important?"

Channel: Bro. Sanchez TV

https://www.youtube.com/watch?v=YLiWO786Wps

Description: I.Q. BUILDERS: NEW Flat Earth Info! by Allegedly Dave Moor in Macedonia (summary) - Originally Edited & posted by "Pi" on Facebook. SHOUT OUT TO IQ BUILDERS. MILENKO & DAVE MURPHY! NEW Flat Earth information by Allegedly Dave Moor speaking in Macedonia! On Macedonian National Television on the Late Night with Milenko show about flat earth proofs in Macedonia. This show is apparently the most popular current affairs program in the country...

NASA Fakery

**FLAT BASTARD ASKS NEIL ARMSTRONG –
"DID YE' REALLY GO TO THE MOON? - FLAT EARTH**

Channel: Flat Bastard

https://www.youtube.com/watch?v=Wods_TaT5_U

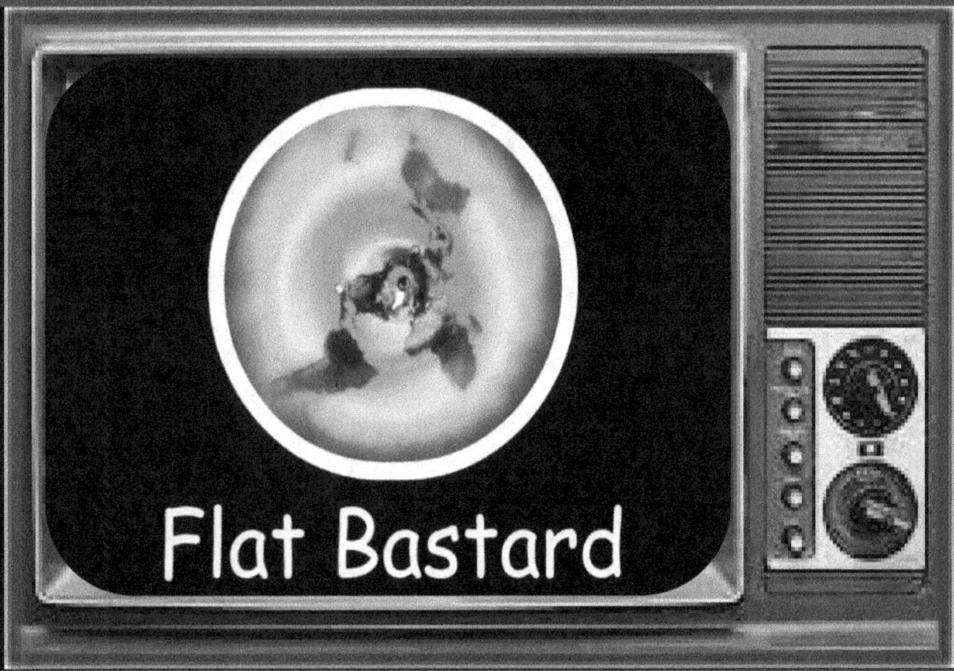

**Description: Flat Earth Maps can be purchased here -
https://www.ebay.com/usr/flat-earth-worldwide**

NASA Fakery

Flat Earth - ISS Studio Exposed

Channel: Flat Earth Hub

https://www.youtube.com/watch?v=7HF_1N77BzM&t=1s

Description: This is additional information pertaining to the recent blue screen being caught by members of the community! Please watch the entire clip, the first bit is from other youtubers but the main clip of new evidence is in the body of the clip, also at the end, make sure to pause and study the glitch I point out!

NASA Fakery

FLAT EARTH ANTARCTIC BALLOON SATELLITE PROGRAMS?!?

Channel: UnsilentMajorityTV

https://www.youtube.com/watch?v=_pJ7JCXLdEk

Description: All the evidence is pointing South. It's time to go South and find out what the global elite scum have been hiding from everyone. The earth is flat, we don't live on a spinning ball! Remember the saying or idiom for when things go bad? You know.. "everything went South" ..lol this is a common saying for when things go downhill. Well yes, for the global elite.. it's BAD.. REALLY BAD for business..FOR THEIR AGENDA .. if WE THE PEOPLE go South!

NASA Fakery

Industrial Valve Expert: The ISS is a LIE - Flat Earth

Channel: 7th Day Truth Seeker

https://www.youtube.com/watch?v=3mBOnHS7de4&t=4614s

Description: Expert Series : Flat Earth : Mark Sargent (link to markksargent video playlist). Statement from Industrial Valve Expert is read concerning the ISS, while Navy Missile Instructor Shaun McCrary joins the discussion. Thank you to Mark Sargent for his kind permission to post this video. Originally Published on Oct 14, 2015 by markksargent

NASA Fakery

ISS Space Station hoax yes the ISS and pretty much everything else to do with NASA

Channel: Steve Blakey

https://www.youtube.com/watch?v=Kgt3V-2xPFU&t=7s

Description: ISS Space Station hoax yes the iss and pretty much everything else to do with NASA

NASA Fakery

NASA = FAKE - Freemasons Busted ISS Space Travel Hoax – Mega Compilation #1

Channel: Roger Ritchey

https://www.youtube.com/watch?v=E0ynuusdjxY

Description: No comment

NASA Fakery

NASA ADMITS THE EARTH IS FLAT WE LIED SORRY! DON PETIT !! MUST SEE

Channel: Rv Truth Over Tradition

https://www.youtube.com/watch?v=MOeSTdhxd4M

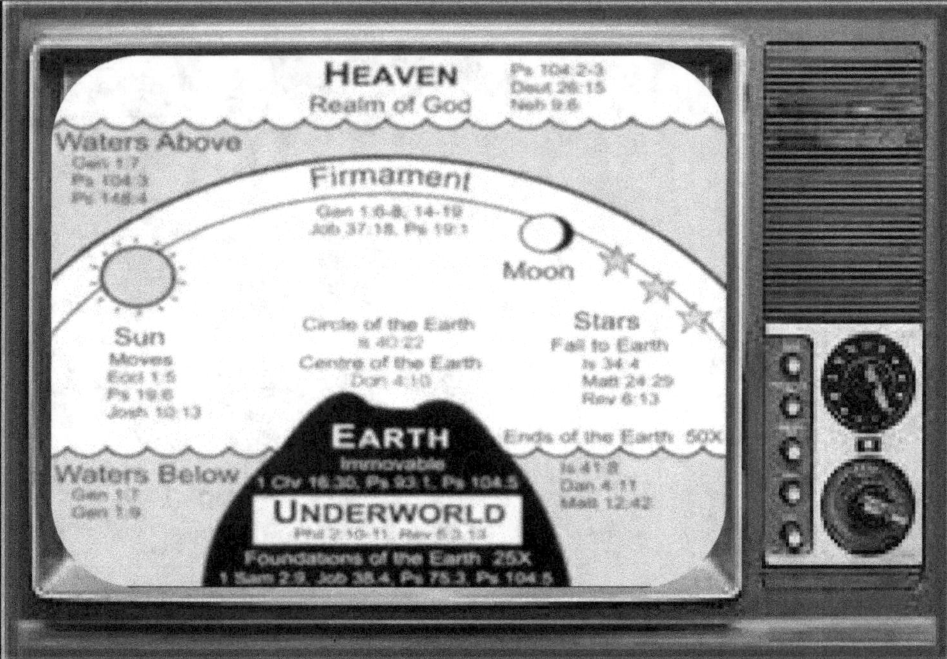

Description: Copyright Disclaimer Under Section 107 of the Copyright Act 1976 - Credit to whoever owns it for the video clips. The use of these clips is not to undermine the copyright that whoever owns it has on this fight but to educate and engage the audience in what really transpired during the event. Thank you.

NASA Fakery

NASA Challenger HOAX crew still alive

Channel: Try Thinking For Once

https://www.youtube.com/watch?v=EFUJW1r6YVo

Description: No comment

NASA Fakery

No human has ever left earth on a rocket by Don Pettit [NASA]?

Channel: PLANATE VERITAS

https://www.youtube.com/watch?v=E7BD6ujljzk&t=7s

Description: No comment

NASA Fakery

Space is fake? SHUT THE FRONT SPACE DOOR!! (Flat Earth Proof)

Channel: the Truth is stranger than fiction...

https://www.youtube.com/watch?v=WTzF2mgBRLk&t=402s

Description: Let's talk about airlocks, both in Hollywood an in "reality"...

NASA Fakery

This is EXACTLY how NASA fakes everything

Channel: Flat Earth Talk

https://www.youtube.com/watch?v=V-Y6CvkEHvc

Description: A technical breakdown of the ISS and how NASA fakes their footage from there. This video is great description of how they fool the masses through technology, specifically called VR or Augmented VR. VR is an abbreviation for virtual reality. This video proof and documented record is by Mike Helmick.

NASA Fakery

Was the moon landing a Hoax ? Wiki leaks tells all ?
Are you ready for the truth ?

Channel: Divine wisdom

https://www.youtube.com/watch?v=tLdR9Jy4F-8

Description: CHECK OUT DIVINE WISDOM FOR NEWS SCIENCE, MYTHOLOGY, LIFE, CULTURE VIDEOS a lot of people are claiming that the moon landing was fake ! do you believe it or not ?

NASA Fakery

What will it take for you to finally admit that we never went to the moon?

Channel: Rob Skiba

https://www.youtube.com/watch?v=4kQ3ma-pdpM

Description: This video contains just a few of MANY reasons which prove we never went to the moon. How much more proof do you require? And if we never went to the moon, they we never got that pic of the Earth from them either. Food for thought.

No Forests on Flat Earth

No Forests on Flat Earth

Ancient mining and forest clearing grid

Channel: Philipp Druzhinin

https://www.youtube.com/watch?v=qekhQU2ahCo

Description: We can observe a whole bunch of different forest clearing grid all around the world. But why we see in the middle of nowhere? They say it was made for some gas exploration, and they use it to sensor the seismic explosions to get the 3d map of the area. Lets find out what I saw on my friends pictures. Much of what I'm showing occurred in the not so distant past as we are led to believe

No Forests on Flat Earth

Colossal ancient Earthworks in America – p 8 / When the Survivors Wake Up

Channel: newearth

https://www.youtube.com/watch?v=SCTrF-mqYLw

Description: Please kindly do not send any youtube messages - those will not be read by Sylvie Ivanova. The only way to contact her is through the contact options on megaliths.org or the forum mentioned above.

No Forests on Flat Earth

Flat Earth - Ancient Tree - Giants - Emerald City & More

Channel: Turquoise Dragon

https://www.youtube.com/watch?v=ER12_XeWcwg

Description: Flat Earth - Ancient Tree - Giants & More   History of the relationship between Man and Nature. religious stories and mythologies. The map shown in the Emerald City also. The Tree of Life, World Tree   Did we destroy the last few remaining "giant trees" on earth, or are these small in comparison to what once flourished here in ancient times not so long ago.

No Forests on Flat Earth

Flat Earth Talk & No Forrests On Flat Earth

Channel: MrThriveAndSurvive

https://www.youtube.com/watch?v=FzHuhuobiQ8

Description: A flat earth talk to set the narrative straight...
There is no reason for a flat earther to have to prove anything. The
burden of proof is not on you. My thoughts on "No Forrests On Flat
Earth"

No Forests on Flat Earth

Flat Earth, Basalt Columns & the Lost Trees of Old...

Channel: the Truth is stranger than fiction...

https://www.youtube.com/watch?v=pf3vE8fZdXU

Description: Flat Earth - Ancient Tree - Giants & More   History of the relationship between Man and Nature. religious stories and mythologies. The map shown in the Emerald City also. The Tree of Life, World Tree   Did we destroy the last few remaining "giant trees" on earth, or are these small in comparison to what once flourished here in ancient times not so long ago.

No Forests on Flat Earth

Flat Earth: Giant Electric Trees

Channel: Aaron Dover

https://www.youtube.com/watch?v=j5qwbB1ftsA

To recap some of my previous videos.

The energy generation industry is a huge fraud
and there is no crude oil or other "fossil fuels". Nor
were there any dinosaurs to slowly melt and become
oil. Our mains electricity seems to be
be harvested from the air at tall towers and by
lengthy isolated power lines across the countryside. Also
there used to be giant trees.

Description: No comment

No Forests on Flat Earth

Giant Tree Stumps in Taiwan, and Asia. No trees on flat earth. My examples and speculations.

Channel: 弋張

https://www.youtube.com/watch?v=LFFOklnz94Q

Description: Giant Tree Stumps in Taiwan, and a neighboring country. There are no trees on flat earth. My examples and speculations.

No Forests on Flat Earth

Gulf of Mexico was a Giant Mining Quarry

Channel: SoulVoice

https://www.youtube.com/watch?v=2z8kSoVCQ8o

Description: Like No Forest on Earth. Evidence shows that, Gulf of Mexico was nothing but a mining quarry for aliens.

Check out the original author of No Forest on Earth

No Forests on Flat Earth

MOUNTAINS ARE DEAD GIANT TREES ON FLAT EARTH PLANE!!!

Channel: subphotonic

https://www.youtube.com/watch?v=747mCkZtDu8

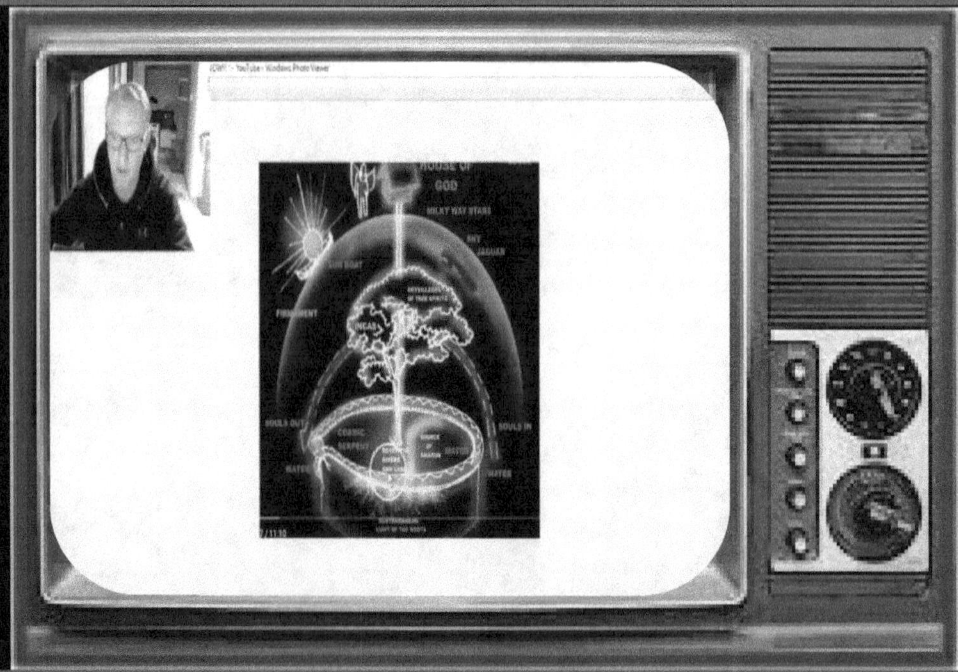

Description: MOUNTAINS ARE DEAD GIANT TREES!!!

No Forests on Flat Earth

No Forests on Flat Earth - New Evidence - Toltec pottery

Channel: Vlad Hangan

https://www.youtube.com/watch?v=1-v-PEi5OaE

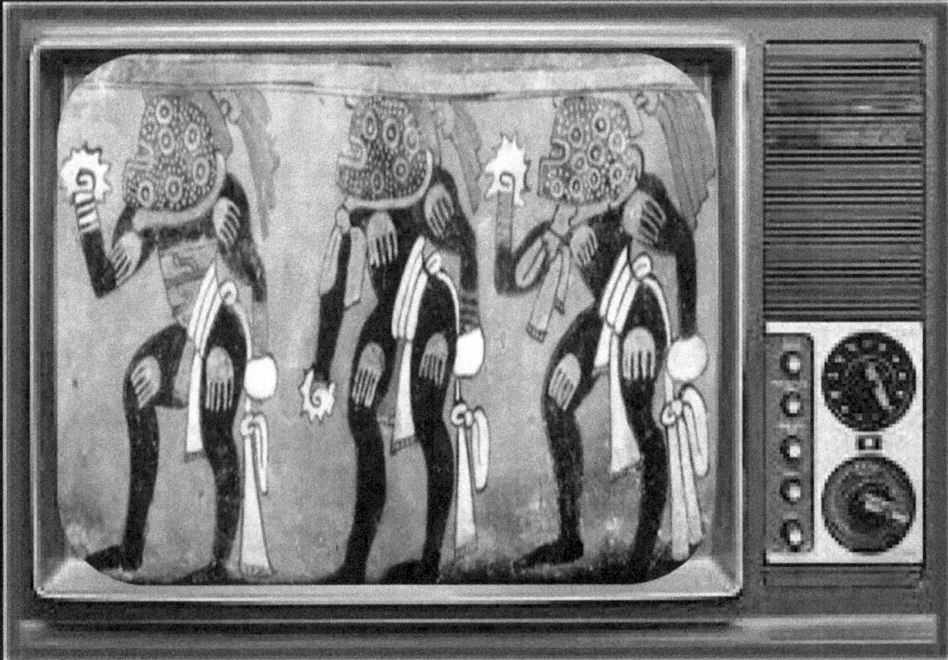

Description: My short video Reaction to No forests on Flat Earth video
as well as presenting some new evidence supporting the idea of Earth
being one giant quarry since ancient times. A little journey to the
ancient South America. Thanks very much.

TOP 201 CONSPIRACY THEORY VIDEOS ON YOUTUBE

No Forests on Flat Earth

No Forests on the Flat Earth RESPONSE (Kent Hovind & the Pre-Flood World) Giant TREES, Giant HUMANS!

Channel: scrawny2brawny

https://www.youtube.com/watch?v=6wFm4rZbNhw

Description: With this video resonating so strongly amongst so many people, I felt it necessary to include my own personal response to the video titled "There are no forests on the flat earth". It was certainly a powerful video, but is it the truth? Let's investigate! Original video: "There are no forests on Flat Earth Wake Up"
https://youtu.be/UHkiZNT3cyE

No Forests on Flat Earth

THE REASON There Are No Forests On Earth Pt 1

Channel: The Last Relevant Sage

https://www.youtube.com/watch?v=Gjap-5b1Pvs

Description: An alternative look at the popular video "There are no forests on flat Earth". English voiceover version
https://youtu.be/ObJL6aA2czo

No Forests on Flat Earth

There are no forests on earth! (English dubbed)

Channel: DITRH

https://www.youtube.com/watch?v=fFrLkNrATGA

Description: READ BEFORE COMMENTING!   This channel does NOT agree 100% with everything said in this video such as what nukes are. The narrator did a live read from the original video and narrated word for word keeping the creators exact narration. We are fully aware if you do a 360 you are right back where you started from. Everyone is aware there are large areas of trees that we call forests however they do not compare to what forests really were.

No Forests on Flat Earth

There are no forests on Flat Earth author interview

Channel: Philipp Druzhinin

https://www.youtube.com/watch?v=npZuIg8de8Y

Description: There are no forests on Flat Earth author interview

Interview with David from Vladivostok Russia.

No Forests on Flat Earth

There are No Forests on Flat Earth Decoded (Part 4) Know Them By Their Fruits 🍊

Channel: rosette delacroix

https://www.youtube.com/watch?v=WTLm53LNo6s

Description: This is Part 4 in my series There are No Forests on Flat Earth Decoded. This one goes into where what the Giant Spheres really are and who is involved in their cover up.

For the read my written article here:
http://rosettedelacroix.com/?p=9759

No Forests on Flat Earth

What you need to know about
GIANT ANCIENT TREE STUMPS... you won't believe it!

Channel: WoodwardTV

https://www.youtube.com/watch?v=n5SRkkhUG4k&t=92s

Description: This topic gained popularity after the release of a
documentary by a Russian author who goes by the name David.
This is my personal review of this theory that originated years ago.
To gain a better understanding of this you MUST watch "There are no
forest on Earth" or "There are no forest on flat earth."
There are no forests on Flat Earth Wake Up:
http://youtu.be/UHkiZNT3cyE

Nuclear Hoax

Nuclear Hoax

Galen Winsor - The Grand Nuclear Hoax

Channel: Mr Grimv

https://www.youtube.com/watch?v=LEXG7h6kBOQ&t=57s

Description: We are dying though so if not by nuclear radiation.., then what?
Vaccines and chemtrails.. more to be seen on this later..
Thanks for thinking with me and take care!

Nuclear Hoax

HIROSHIMA: WHAT REALLY HAPPENED? Nuclear truth *NO GRAPHICS* Rerevisionist & John Friend

Channel: rerevisionist

https://www.youtube.com/watch?v=GA8kJaP2m1w

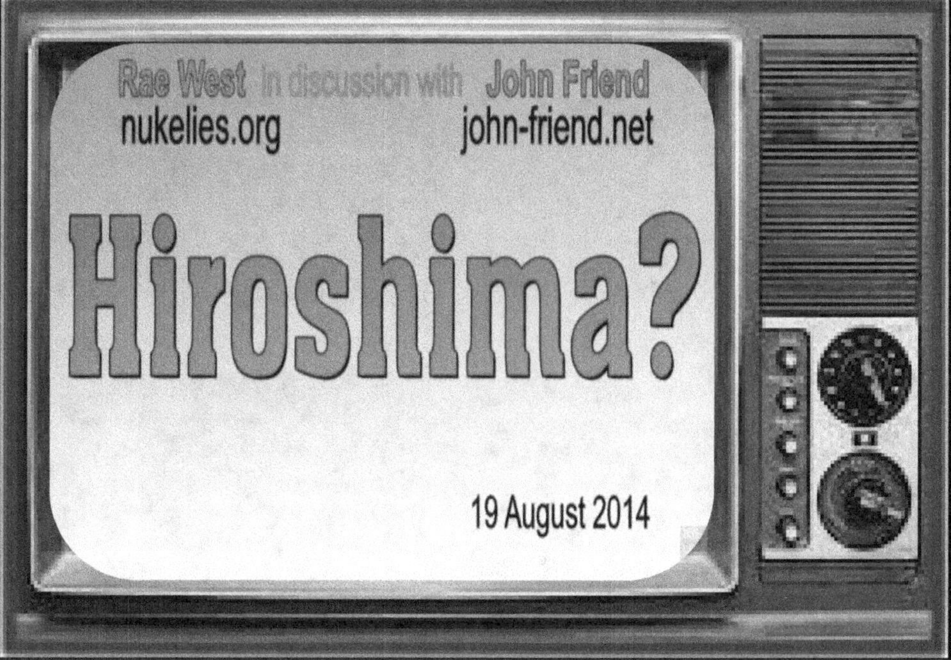

Description: Hiroshima bombing. What really happened at Hiroshima?
Long video is Nukes Don't Exist
https://www.youtube.com/watch?v=UHjohmgOh2M
Firestorm over Hiroshima - Rerevisionist & John Friend discuss the
evidence, showing there was no atom bomb. (2 Youtube versions)

Nuclear Hoax

Nuclear Hoax - Nukes Do Not Exist!

Channel: Eric Dubay

https://www.youtube.com/watch?v=sULjMjK5lCI&t=4753s

Description: The following documentary explores the truth about nuclear energy and the surprisingly abundant evidence that nuclear weapons are a hoax. Many of the nuclear explosion videos we have all seen and presumed real are shown to be complete fakes using model trees, houses and cars exploding on a set. The destruction of Hiroshima and Nagasaki were not the result of one large explosion as advertised, but rather the result of a fire-bombing campaign comparable to Tokyo's

Nuclear Hoax

Nuclear Weapons Do Not Exist - Made in Hollywood!

Channel: MrE

https://www.youtube.com/watch?v=6NEcIQk2UjA

Description: Lookout Mountain Laboratories in Hollywood was a secret state of the art Air Force film studio that made nuclear testing films. Many of these images are simply close-ups of the sun with color saturation and cross faded to give the illusion of movement. Others are conventional explosions with a fake layer of clouds that appear too close to the ground to give the illusion of height.

Nuclear Hoax

NUCLEAR WEAPONS DO NOT EXIST
The Documentary By Edmund Matthews

Channel: EdmundMatthewsTVOW

https://www.youtube.com/watch?v=jo7Ytg9ckC0&t=2398s

Description: NUCLEAR WEAPONS DON'T EXIST The Documentary By Edmund Matthews http://www.edmundmatthews.com/

Nuclear Hoax

THE NUCLEAR HOAX

Channel: theTRUman

https://www.youtube.com/watch?v=M-GliAMA-3c&t=925s

Description: originally uploaded by channel "Dorje Daka" titled "No Fear No Nuclear War ✓"
original upload link;
https://www.youtube.com/watch?v=AtbzOI25szQ&feature=youtu.be
original channel link;
https://www.youtube.com/channel/UC9i9EoI550riSIgMlpuTm-w

Secret Societies

Secret Societies

97% Owned - Economic Truth documentary – Queuepolitely cut

Channel: QueuePolitely

https://www.youtube.com/watch?v=XcGh1Dex4Yo

Description: Watch the sequel:
https://www.youtube.com/watch?v=p5Ac7ap_MAY

97% owned present serious research and verifiable evidence on our economic and financial system. This is the first documentary to tackle this issue from a UK-perspective and explains the inner workings of Central Banks and the Money creation process.

TOP 201 CONSPIRACY THEORY VIDEOS ON YOUTUBE

Secret Societies

Aleister Crowley, the Wickedest Man in the World Explained in 5 Minutes

Channel: reallygraceful

https://www.youtube.com/watch?v=KZeoZfeAdIw

Description: This is an introduction to Aleister Crowley, the Beast 666, in five minutes. Of course, we're only skimming the surface of Crowley's life and work.

TOP 201 CONSPIRACY THEORY VIDEOS ON YOUTUBE

Secret Societies

ALEX JONES INFO WARS OWNED BY TIME WARNER CABLE!

Channel: Rv Truth Over Tradition

https://www.youtube.com/watch?v=TVb4XSr5Egk

Description: Credit to whoever owns it for the video clips. The use of these clips is not to undermine the copyright that whoever owns it has on this fight but to educate and engage the audience in what really transpired during the event. Thank you.

Secret Societies

ALEX JONES IS BILL HICKS PART 1

Channel: Plymouth Fury

https://www.youtube.com/watch?v=H4ORdUZRi04

Description: 15 reasons why Bill Hicks and Alex Jones are the same person. It's the combination of factors which makes this allegation a certainty.

Secret Societies

Banksters, Gangsters & the New World Order
Federal Reserve Documentary ▶

Channel: ODD Reality

https://www.youtube.com/watch?v=GnYDeHosREs

Description: This is dedicated to all the Zionist Jew Banksters and the Illuminati Gangsters. The crooks of the Federal Reserve System. The spiderweb network that's consists of the Council on Foreign Relations (CFR), the Bilderberg Group, The International Monetary Fund (IMF), the United Nations (U.N), the Trilateral Commission, Bohemian Club, Skull & Bones, Freemasons, House of Rothschild, House of Rockefeller, Royal Institute for International Affairs, Club of Rome, the Tavistock Institute...

Secret Societies

Bill Hicks in 1994 Playing the Character Alex Jones

Channel: Skippy hereitcomesskippy

https://www.youtube.com/watch?v=p2dC0p7d9do

Description: He didn't have the fake voice worked out yet in 1994. That was his first year playing the character of "Alex Jones".

TOP 201 CONSPIRACY THEORY VIDEOS ON YOUTUBE

Secret Societies

CELL TOWERS: "5G", Verizon ILLUMINATi TAKEOVER, FREEMASON MEDIA COLOR CODES!!

Channel: The Black Child

https://www.youtube.com/watch?v=kPrc7rK0--U

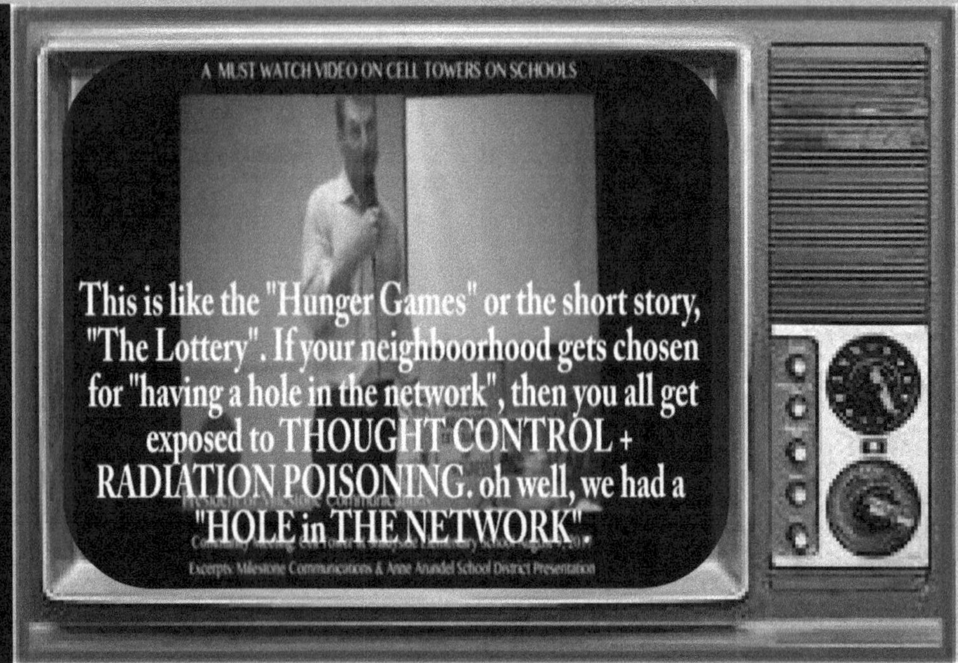

Description: CELL TOWERS: FREEMASON- ILLUMINATi "News Media" COLOR CODING; Verizon NATIONWIDE TAKEOVER; "5G"; "Cell Towers 2017!!"

Secret Societies

CHARLIE SHEEN: Satanic Freak Pedophile EXPOSED AGAIN!!!!!!

Channel: The Black Child

https://www.youtube.com/watch?v=vDpubIlI6H0

Description: Someone confirms what this channel reported EXCLUSIVELY back in 2014, that Charlie Sheen raped Corey Haim in the 80's. What are the implications for Alex Jones & Infowars??

Secret Societies

Donald Trump Was Trained By Jesuits - The World's A Stage

Channel: FlatWater FlatEarth

https://www.youtube.com/watch?v=y0BIR9seQTg

Description: Donald J. Trump ... the anti-establishment hero, chosen by the establishment. Trump has major ties to insider banking elites in New York, and is indisputably trained by the Jesuits. This means that the (s)elections in the United States, the Republican / Democrat deception, is only about the illusion of choice. Rome has been ruling undercover (through banking) for some 150 years. The Rothschilds just "guard" the Papal Treasure, they don't own the treasure.

Secret Societies

Esoteric Freemasonry: The 33rd Degree.

Channel: Illuminati Zeitgeist!

https://www.youtube.com/watch?v=WiP6MskQlF4

Description: WOEIH #60 Esoteric Freemasonry and the 33rd Degree explained.
http://www.WhatOnEarthIsHappening.com   WOEIH Show #060: 5/15/2011 Mark Passio from the What On Earth Is Happening radio show continues the discussion of Esoteric Freemasonry with the discussion of Scottish Rite 32 and 33 degree symbols, the illumined degrees, reverse of the Great Seal and the Great Work.

Secret Societies

Flat Earth: Jesuits & the Global Conspiracy!

Channel: WLC Videos

https://www.youtube.com/watch?v=1WHIr-IFqAo

Description: Coincidences of dates, agendas, and goals, connect the Jesuits to a massive deception over the true shape of the earth – all for the purpose of a multi-faceted end time delusion. • The Earth is flat. • The Earth is not a globe. • Copernicus & Galileo: the Hegelian Dialectic • From the Nazis to NASA: the Vatican rules... • Jesuits & The Counter Reformation • "LUCIFER" & the Coming of Christ

Secret Societies

FOUR Signs of an Illuminati Hit.

Channel: The Black Child

https://www.youtube.com/watch?v=2G_oi_PiTvE

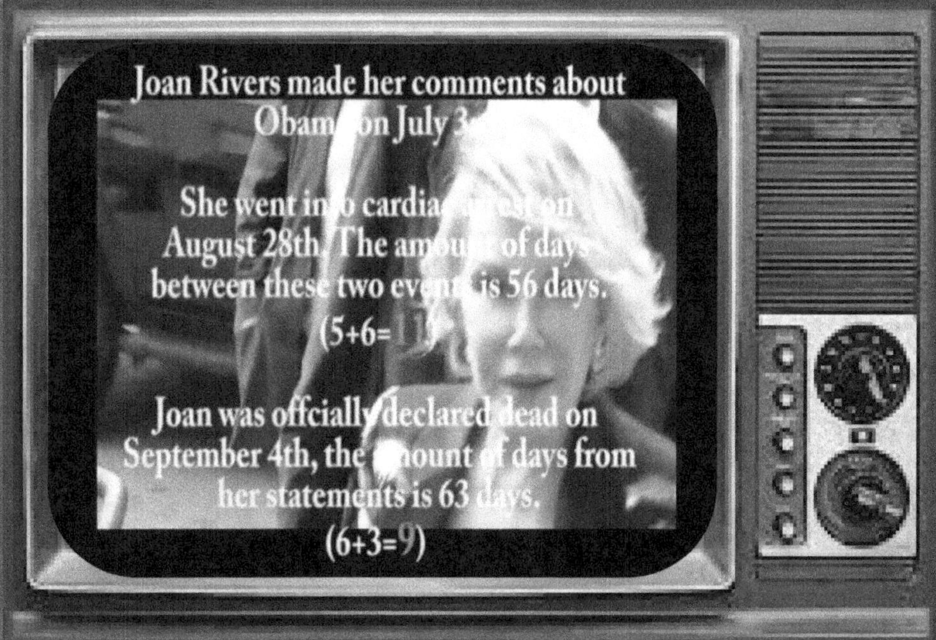

Description: Thanks to Yash Qaraah of 7stage.com

Secret Societies

Freemasonry Secrets From Their Books Of The Masonic Order

Channel: opening the matrix

https://www.youtube.com/watch?v=0prMkcGraw0

Description: No comment

Secret Societies

Historical Origins Of The Jesuit Order. The Diabolical Society Of Jesus & Knights Of Malta Exposed!

Channel: End Times Prophecies & Events

https://www.youtube.com/watch?v=iBLwBlqjLSs

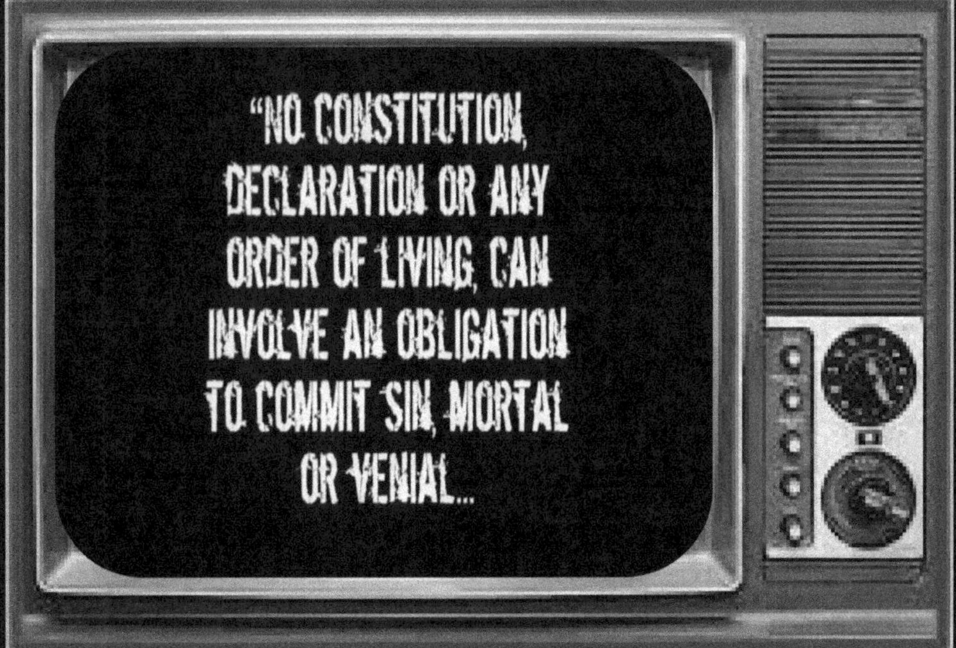

Description: Historical Origins Of The Jesuit Order. The Diabolical Society Of Jesus, Knights Of Malta, Catholicism, Freemasonry, & The Occult/Esoteric Exposed! Pope Francis Exposed An Antichrist & False Prophet! Vladimir Putin, Barack Obama, & The Leaders Of The World Are Secretly Working Together Behind Closed Doors. God Bless & Jesus Saves.

Secret Societies

House of Windsor and the New World Order

Channel: bluesmovers

https://www.youtube.com/watch?v=N33BtgpscUE

Description: Tried to fix the worst audio sync problems, and re-uploaded from another channel. People need to know this information.

Secret Societies

Illuminati Exposed | Masquerade Ball & Sex Magick ▶

Channel: ODD Reality

https://www.youtube.com/watch?v=6IcbkkVNEB0

Description: Hey guys. ODD here. I've been having these thoughts about the Illuminati / Surrealist Ball and I wanted to dive in with you all. I know for a fact that it's all about the sex magick aspect and I did my best here to prove my point. I was going to do my normal style of video, but I decided "Hey. Why not freestyle a video every once in a while." So this is raw, but I'm sure you'll learn a thing or two here. Thanks for watching.

Secret Societies

JFK Secret Societies Speech (full version)

Channel: MrMnmn911

https://www.youtube.com/watch?v=zdMbmdFOvTs&t=4s

Description: Was JFK's comment on "secret societies" a statement against the "NWO"? I searched this famous quote and finally found the full unedited written transcript and audio of this speech. JFK was actually talking about current events of the cold war and how nontraditional enemies were gaining information on how the US was battling this war. In this speech JFK actually points out "the need for far greater "official" secrecy"...as well as "the need for a far greater public...

Secret Societies

Krs One - Explains the Illuminati, Freemasons, and if he's a member

Channel: beatGrade

https://www.youtube.com/watch?v=IZqghCSEj94

Description: The Full Interview of Krs One, we ask him if he is a member of the secret societies known as the Freemasons, the Illuminati, and his thoughts. beatGrade is a music news source and media website for discovering talent and sharing music. New videos added weekly to our channel. Subscribe now for the latest updates, performances, interviews, and music from new and established artists. http://www.beatgrade.com/

Secret Societies

List of Freemason Celebrities: The Brotherhood

Channel: Dayz of Noah

https://www.youtube.com/watch?v=eYLyJvgpKLo

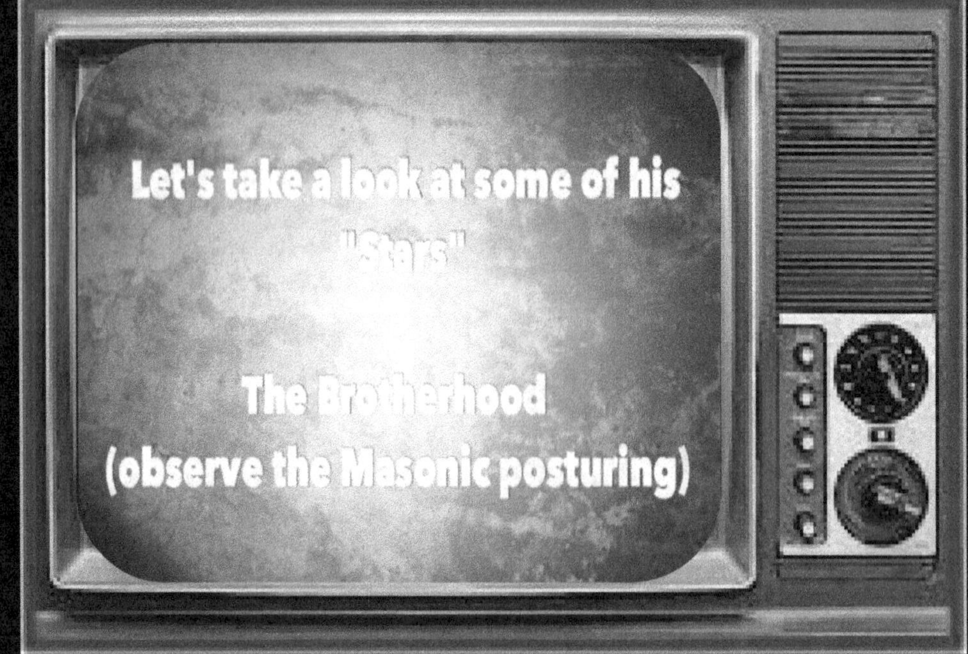

Description: Taking a glance at some key figures played on the black and white chessboard. Though many blue lodge/low level Masons are oblivious to the workings of the Masonic Orders, the overall network and power structure of Masonry provides the foundation for the One World Govt and New World Order.

Secret Societies

M3dia Mock3ry - Alex Jones aka Bill Hicks Fakes An "Assault" On TV

Channel: TSRTHESILENTREVOLUTION1988

https://www.youtube.com/watch?v=6dGKsMWDSvw

Description: Truth Is In Th3 Numb3rs
Paypal: darthh8r@protonmail.com
Resources: http://www.gematrinator.com/calculator/index.php
http://masonicdictionary.com/numbers.html
http://www.crystalinks.com/numerology4.html

Secret Societies

Mystery of the Widow's Son - The Legend of the Craft

Channel: michaelrose93

https://www.youtube.com/watch?v=dvUNRekfEE8&t=689s

Description: Hiram Abiff was busy working his Craft, when he suddenly found himself transported into the center of the Earth by Tubal-Cain, there to taste of the Tree of Knowledge. . . Who was the original 'Widow's Son'? That all depends on who you ask. This documentary explores a particular thread of Masonic history, namely the origin of the third degree, and the 'lineage' of the Craft.

Secret Societies

Occulted Anatomy: Masonic Symbolism, Arc of the Covenant, the Brain/ Universe

Channel: Lifting The Veil / Cullen Smith

https://www.youtube.com/watch?v=UIkoVsmVK9A

Description: This is an excerpt from my full video presentation series "Symbols Of Power pt 2" which you can watch here https://www.patreon.com/posts/symbols... in which I syncretize many esoteric truths about the human body and how it is symbolically portrayed as the foundational basis of mythology, theology, language and so much more! This clip has excluded the sexuality and other mature themes from the presentation.

Secret Societies

Psywar - Full Documentary

Channel: Conspiracy Documentaries

https://www.youtube.com/watch?v=2eB046f998U&t=3569s

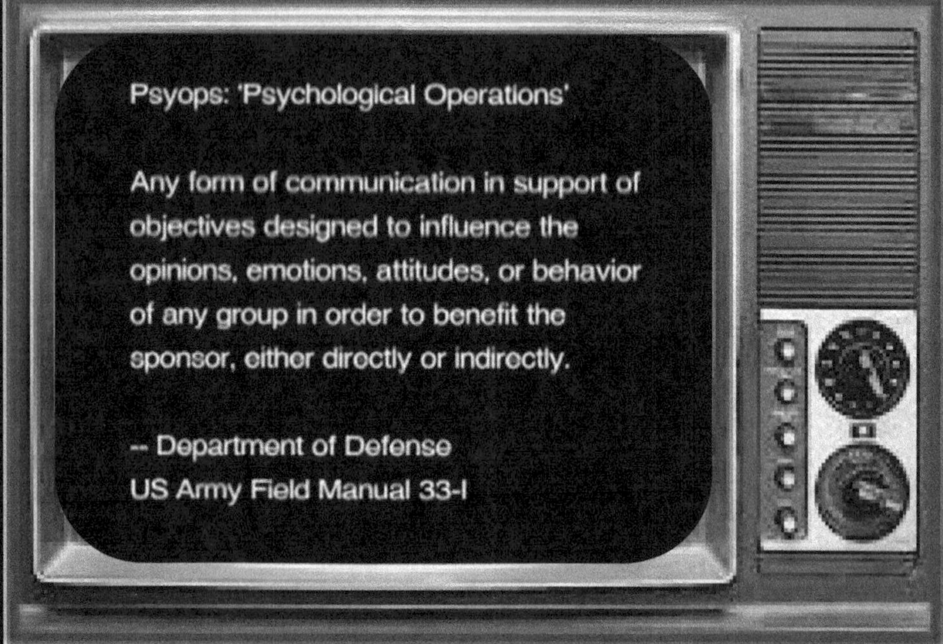

Description: See more at http://www.ConspiracyDocumentaries.com
This film explores the evolution of propaganda and public relations in
the United States, with an emphasis on the "elitist theory of
democracy" and the relationship between war, propaganda and class.
Includes original interviews with a number of dissident scholars
including Noam Chomsky, Howard Zinn, Michael Parenti, Peter Phillips
("Project Censored"), John Stauber ("PR Watch")...

Secret Societies

Rick and Morty 9/11 Truth Hidden In Plain Sight - Illuminati

Channel: Killuminati Vids

https://www.youtube.com/watch?v=EPuBfHIex4o

Description: EDIT: I agree, it does sound more like "It's an excuse to strip away our freedoms." Just wanted to make that correction. Rick, who obviously time travels, saw 9/11 for what it truly was. He is seen in this episode, saying the phrase "It's an excuse that took away our freedom." 9/11 was an obvious inside job now that we look at it with new eyes... But amazing how Rick knew what it was from the moment it happened. Terrorism is a lie. The government committed treason on that very day.

Secret Societies

Secrets in Plain Sight Documentary

Channel: DoUSEEwhatEYEC

https://www.youtube.com/watch?v=Ocleaf0NDqo&t=162s

Description: Reuploaded from
https://www.youtube.com/user/Secretsinplainsight
No money made from this video..sharing for educational purposes.

Secret Societies

The Boule , Black Greek Fraternities , Illuminati Freemason Celebrities Exposed! PT. 1

Channel: Bro. Sanchez TV

https://www.youtube.com/watch?v=m7ppgU5KBWE

Description: Your world is a stage and everything you see and hear is designed to further indoctrinate you, program your mind and to serve an agenda. The matrix is real. What do you believe and why? Who programmed you with your current values? Who gave you the "history" that is determining your future and is it real? Black history, black media, crisis actors, Prince Hall Maonry, hip hop occult and so many more have a played vital roles in conditioning your mind and serving the divide...

Secret Societies

THE DEATH OF DONALD TRUMP: PREDICTIVE PROGRAMMING! The Simpsons' most Creepy Prediction!

Channel: IMMINENT Rapture REPENT

https://www.youtube.com/watch?v=QRxiYfLjogs

Description: Daniel 11: 20
 20 Then shall stand up in his estate a raiser of taxes in the glory of the kingdom: but within FEW DAYS he SHALL BE DESTROYED, neither in anger, nor in battle. (Trump)
 21 And in his estate shall stand up a vile person, to whom they shall not give the honour of the kingdom: but he shall come in peaceably, and obtain the kingdom by flatteries.

Secret Societies

The Greatest Kept Secret of Freemasonry REVEALED!

Channel: D13 Watchmen

https://www.youtube.com/watch?v=BLL0X_-Z1OE

Description: What do the Masons know about Earths design? Now you will know their secret. The Garden of Eden and the North revealed.

Secret Societies

The History Of The Turkish Khazars People

Channel: MadeInTurkey

https://www.youtube.com/watch?v=ORz2nOcOTyQ

Description: The Khazars (Turkish: Hazarlar, Tatar: Xäzärlär, Hebrew: כוזרים‎Kuzarim), Arabic: خزر‎) khazar), Russian: Хазары, Persian: خزر‎ , Greek: Χάζαροι, Latin: Gazari /Cosri /Gasani) were a semi-nomadic Turkic people who created what for its duration was the most powerful polity to emerge from the breakup of the western Turkish steppe empire, known as the Khazar Khanate or Khazaria.

Secret Societies

The Jesuits Plan to Rule the World (in progress)

Channel: Elliott Hall

https://www.youtube.com/watch?v=rYV7RiAOFis

Description: Check out Johnny Cirucci
https://www.youtube.com/user/THEJohnnyCirucci for better
information. This video doesn't tell the whole truth. Eric John Phelps is
a liar telling half-truths. Giovanni Augustino Cirucci ("Johnny") wrote 3
weighty books on Jesuits.

Secret Societies

The Khazarian Conspiracy –
The Synagogue of Satan - Full Movie

Channel: TIME TO RISE AGAIN

https://www.youtube.com/watch?v=dikhbqzF-Sg

Description: I coudn't find a better resolution version. Also around 53 minutes mark the footage skips. I think it is because of copyrights claims. Every other version I uploaded have been blocked.

Secret Societies

The Luciferian Doctrine in America

Channel: TheRapeOfJustice

https://www.youtube.com/watch?v=aV3oDXHzU3U&t=145s

Description: Anthony Hilder and William David Cox touring through Hanford CA, and Lemoore CA, USA, in 2010. On Lucifer, Baphomet, Ba'al, Canaanites, Secret Societies, Satanism, Paganism, Neo-Paganism, Moses Holbrook, Henry Wadsworth Longfellow, Freemasonry, International Order of Odd Fellows, Andrew Carnegie, Bohemian Grove, Walter Cronkite, Harry F. Ward, ACLU, World Council of Churches founded in Amsterdam 1948, America founded by Deists, Rotary Club, Illuminati, O.T.O, The Eastern…

Secret Societies

THE MEANING BEHIND THE "VULCAN" SIGN!

Channel: A Call For An Uprising 2

https://www.youtube.com/watch?v=w3JsoXRBELA

Description: THE MEANING BEHIND THE "VULCAN" SIGN!

Secret Societies

The Most Important Video You Will Ever Watch – The Jesuits, Kingpins Of The Matrix (MIRRORED)

Channel: Insanity is Sanity

https://www.youtube.com/watch?v=-dWhmfopLU0

Description: After watching this show I had to share it with you guys, this information is so important and these guys explained it so well. A lot of great information was crammed in to this 90 minute show so perfectly. A plus point, is that both speakers are Flat Earthers ;) Enjoy. In this show Jamie and Bruce will talk to us about the Jesuits, who they are along with helping us understand the staggering level of power and control they possess and how that influence is used to bring about their world order...

Secret Societies

The Religion of the 21st Century: Scientism "Follow Science Be Smart"

Channel: jeranism

https://www.youtube.com/watch?v=9nxIxj__rCw

Description: Lots of content here. Info re: TIME TO LAUNCH. And all the other flat earth news and updates. Calling out the frauds and getting everyone ready for the next step.? Ready for step 2?

Secret Societies

The Roman Catholic Church
THEY ARE NOT WHO THEY CLAIM TO BE

Channel: End Times Productions

https://www.youtube.com/watch?v=EcInR63AeRY

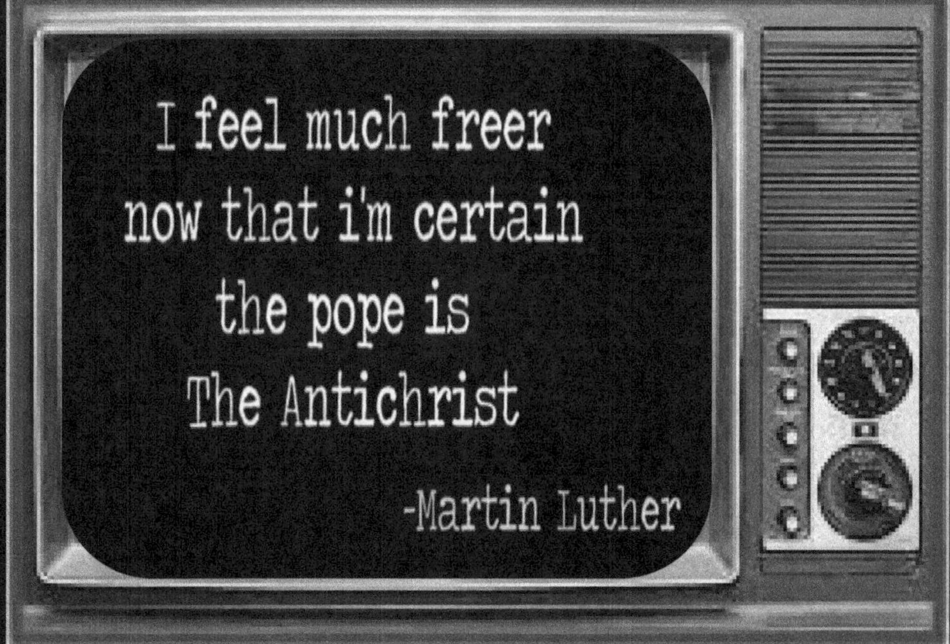

Description: There is something sinister luring beneath the streets of Rome. The Vatican Is hiding its connection to ancient sun-god worship and the mystery religions of Babylon. Special thanks - Steve Quayle Tim Alberino
http://www.stevequayle.com/
www.gen6productions.com
Thank you for watching

Secret Societies

The Secret History of The Khazarian Mafia

Channel: Secret Wars

https://www.youtube.com/watch?v=EmNR8_sTKoo

Secret Societies

The Zionists, Freemasons, and NASA's Biggest Secret

Channel: Eric Dubay

https://www.youtube.com/watch?v=dTqmcvdm4hM&t=1957s

Description: Continuing my discussion with Mel Fabregas of Veritas Radio, we discuss subjects ranging from the Sun, Moon, and stars, UFOs, aliens, and DMT, Jews, Hitler and WWII, and of course, the flat Earth. If you missed part one be sure to watch this first:
https://www.youtube.com/watch?v=5yRAQG5-ca8
And special thanks to Steve Wilner for the awesome psychedelic visuals:
https://www.youtube.com/user/soundlessdawn

Secret Societies

These 100 Secret Societies Prove Who Really Rules America

Channel: Truthstream Media

https://www.youtube.com/watch?v=ON8xq0djCRk

Description: Please support us on Patreon, every bit helps, read our goals here! https://www.patreon.com/truthstreammedia

Truthstream Can Be Found Here:
Website: http://TruthstreamMedia.com

Secret Societies

Untold Truth About African Americans - You Are Not From Africa

Channel: Dane Calloway

https://www.youtube.com/watch?v=srqdLWwTvKQ

Description: ALL NEW VISITORS CAN SUBSCRIBE TO MY CHANNEL HERE -
(Thumbs up this video!)
http://youtube.com/c/DaneCalloway
HELP SUPPORT MY CHANNEL & CONTENT HERE -
(Contribute to keep this ship sailing & earn rewards!)
http://patreon.com/danecalloway

Secret Societies

Vatican Secret Societies, NWO,
The Devil's General Full Documentary

Channel: Watchman For Truth Victory Of The Light!

https://www.youtube.com/watch?v=B55R2MfGFso

Description: This is an excellent documentary touching on the unknown history of the setting up of the American Colonies, and the influences of the Roman Catholic Church and the Jesuit order in the Establishment of the Sovereign Constitutional Republican Nation States of America. Much of this information will be new to many people who received a classic Government provided education. The truth has been modified by the Society of Jesus and the people indoctrinated via...

Secret Societies

Watch THIS Before Joining Freemasonry!
EVERYTHING EXPOSED BY A 33RD MASON

Channel: UrBrain Wash TV

https://www.youtube.com/watch?v=CI2dNWJZzgg

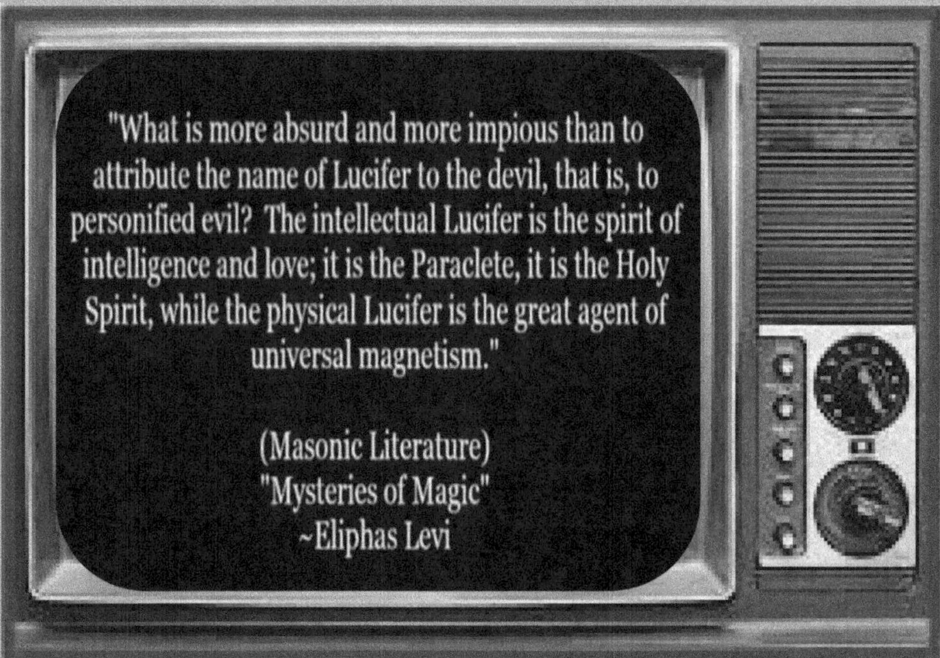

Description: ♥Giving The Video A Like Helps The Channel Grow♥
♥ Subscribe To Us - https://goo.gl/uFgAw8
♥ Visit Our Website - http://urbrainwash.gq

Secret Societies

What you need to know about the
ILLUMINATI CARD GAME...absolute MADNESS!

Channel: WoodwardTV

https://www.youtube.com/watch?v=elrl1UUOKmw

Description: Here I will discuss the Illuminati Card Game. This is a game that has been talked about for years. It has won several game awards in it's day, and there maybe a dark message for all those who look. Secret societies...false flags...non-human entities...political and corporate conspiracies...this game has it all.

Secret Societies

World Secrets - Freemasons, Ancient Egypt,
Knights Templar, Enoch etc.

Channel: Chris K

https://www.youtube.com/watch?v=uk5_o44vars

Description: No comment

Shooting Hoaxes

Shooting Hoaxes

CNN Crisis Actor Caught Red Handed 4 Times In A Row!!! WOW (MUST SEE)

Channel: FastPuma

https://www.youtube.com/watch?v=LM8bwTNN8EE&t=64s

Description: No copyright intended, if you own the rights to this video
and dont want me to use it, please send me a email and i will delete it
right away,
Original uploader is the Pete Santilli show This is about a crisis actor
who has been spotted on camera numorous times. Thanks for watching
Subscribe for more videos ☺

Shooting Hoaxes

crISIS Actors for Dummies - The Females

Channel: Mycousinsfriend Saiditsreal

https://www.youtube.com/watch?v=5QkXNEwGlUE

Description: crISIS Actors for Dummies - The Females   Gabrielle
"Gabby" Giffords - Speaking..Speaking Speaking is Difficult (For Me):
https://www.youtube.com/watch?v=gZToNQtex4s
Gabrielle "Gabby" Giffords - Nothing But Lies! 100% Government
Scripted Lies! - Compilation:
https://www.youtube.com/watch?v=SzNvI3HjrVE
KEEPVID: http://keepvid.com/

Shooting Hoaxes

False Flag Event Exposed (Orlando Shooting)

Channel: The Eliot

https://www.youtube.com/watch?v=hzxk0VizdY0

Description: False Flag Event Exposed (Orlando Shooting) Follow The Eliot On Steemit: https://steemit.com/@the-eliot Make sure you upvote the content!
Follow Our Backup Channel On Vid.Me: https://vid.me/The_Eliot
Subscribe To Our Main Channel:
http://www.youtube.com/c/FreeThePublicTV Like, Subscribe, Share And Comment Below!

Shooting Hoaxes

Fraud Gabby Giffords Gimp Act Exposed

Channel: jeranism

https://www.youtube.com/watch?v=ciBx2ZGyZBg&t=124s

Description: A video to close the door on the fraudulent hoax that is Gabby Giffords. The actual event remains a mystery as none of it makes sense. There is so much wrong with the official story that someone could seriously make a channel just about her and her lying astroNOT or ACTORnaut husband Mark Kelly. Gabrielle Giffords pretends to be mentally challenged and it is all an act. An act of treason! By the way her last name is Hornstein, not Giffords.

Shooting Hoaxes

How Billions were * FOOLED * by the Vegas shooting (redo)

Channel: Nevada Forensics

https://www.youtube.com/watch?v=cndOsUE8yi4

Description: What evidence convinced you that 600 people got this?

Shooting Hoaxes

Las Vegas Shooting - Numerology of the False Flag

Channel: Gematrinator_64

https://www.youtube.com/watch?v=W_qR0X4dIMI&t=1301s

Description: In this video, I expose the numerology of the Las Vegas False Flag shooting from October 1st, 2017. We are in a new information age and the occult no longer has the edge on knowledge. See how this attack was a tribute to the ancient Roman God of trust and good faith, Fides, and its asteroid. Trump is using this attack to push his New World Order anti-gun agenda, and it's time the people of this world stand up and do something to stop these criminals running...

TOP 201 CONSPIRACY THEORY VIDEOS ON YOUTUBE

Shooting Hoaxes

Las Vegas Shooting was a planned Hoax: Part 1

Channel: Rv Truth Over Tradition

https://www.youtube.com/watch?v=lsFkRrJ-fZ8

Description: Credit to whoever owns it for the video clips. The use of these clips is not to undermine the copyright that whoever owns it has on this fight but to educate and engage the audience in what really transpired during the event. Thank you.

Shooting Hoaxes

Mandalay Bay CRISIS ACTORs On Parade

Channel: RichieFromBoston

https://www.youtube.com/watch?v=Vc66hMppH2M

Description: Between Alex jones signing off on the ISIS meme, and the dozens of bullshit fugaze witnesses ALA 911,sandy hook etc etc etc Im not buying it was a shooting at all. It was crisis actors mixed into the audience when the SOUNDS EFFECTS started they dropped like rocks, and thats why there is zero bloody, injured etc footage. RFB

Shooting Hoaxes

New York City psyop

Channel: Rv Truth Over Tradition

https://www.youtube.com/watch?v=YjPicTMwd8s

Description: Credit to whoever owns it for the video clips. The use of these clips is not to undermine the copyright that whoever owns it has on this fight but to educate and engage the audience in what really transpired during the event. Thank you.

Shooting Hoaxes

Only Sandy Hook Video You Need To Show Others/Share!!!

Channel: Robert Zimmerman

https://www.youtube.com/watch?v=I1Qg15bP2jY

Description: See FAIR USE STATEMENT Below... Story 1: "I had no idea at the extent of this tragedy WHEN I GOT TO THE FIREHOUSE. If I had, I don't know that I could'a gotten there. But I did and MY SON thankfully WAS THERE." Story 2: (:34 later) - "MY HUSBAND HAD ALREADY GOTTEN TO THE FIREHOUSE AND PICKED MY SON UP. So, BY THE TIME I GOT down THERE... THEY WERE GONE."

Shooting Hoaxes

Operation Las Vegas - The Breakdown
The International Master Society Program

Channel: Subtle Infinity

https://www.youtube.com/watch?v=d3RFsewb8IM

Description: Operation Las Vegas - The Breakdown Part 2 "The Las Vegas Effect | The Smoking Gun (Cause) & Stream of Holograms (Effect)" https://youtu.be/0FPQJ94Hzbl   To assist in the expansion of this work please Share, Like, Subscribe or click the link below to support, paypal.me/subtleinfinity Your support is greatly appreciated. Peace & Blessings

Shooting Hoaxes

Orlando Nightclub Shooting Spree Hoax – Debunked and Exposed

Channel: MatrixBreak

https://www.youtube.com/watch?v=KRIO1pinRHE

Description: Orlando Shooting Spree - Hoax - Actors Exposed, 6 media corporations control, Exposed Journalists, Sponsorship Propaganda. https://www.youtube.com/watch?v=_qVGvO58DGY Conspiracy song with fake actor images Thanks to wellaware1.com for the greenberg match.

Shooting Hoaxes

Russianvids - Ariana Grande Hoax
More Fake Crying and Real Smiling

Channel: Zack Greevey

https://www.youtube.com/watch?v=UTLUxWx5jM0

Description: Originally Posted by the Legendary Truth Channel - Russianvids.

Shooting Hoaxes

Russianvids BBC News Anchor Live News Blunder Fail Strange Behavior Explained 3 22 17 Skull And

Channel: Zack Greevey

https://www.youtube.com/watch?v=OGhVlDp5v40

Description: Originally Posted by the Legendary Truth Channel - Russianvids.

Shooting Hoaxes

Same Crisis Actors in different occasions

Channel: Gonçalo D

https://www.youtube.com/watch?v=B3OkjZ9Deos

Description: No comment

Shooting Hoaxes

Sandy Hook Actors Playing Dual Rolls??? Busted??

Channel: JimmyEatsWorld

https://www.youtube.com/watch?v=XTNKS-D-Jt0

Description: Crisis actors were used in Sandy Hook without a doubt. But is it possible one of them may have played dual rolls and is now.......BUSTED???

Shooting Hoaxes

SANDY HOOK HOAX IN 6 MINUTES

Channel: Two-Party System

https://www.youtube.com/watch?v=G1Ib8kWMGpw

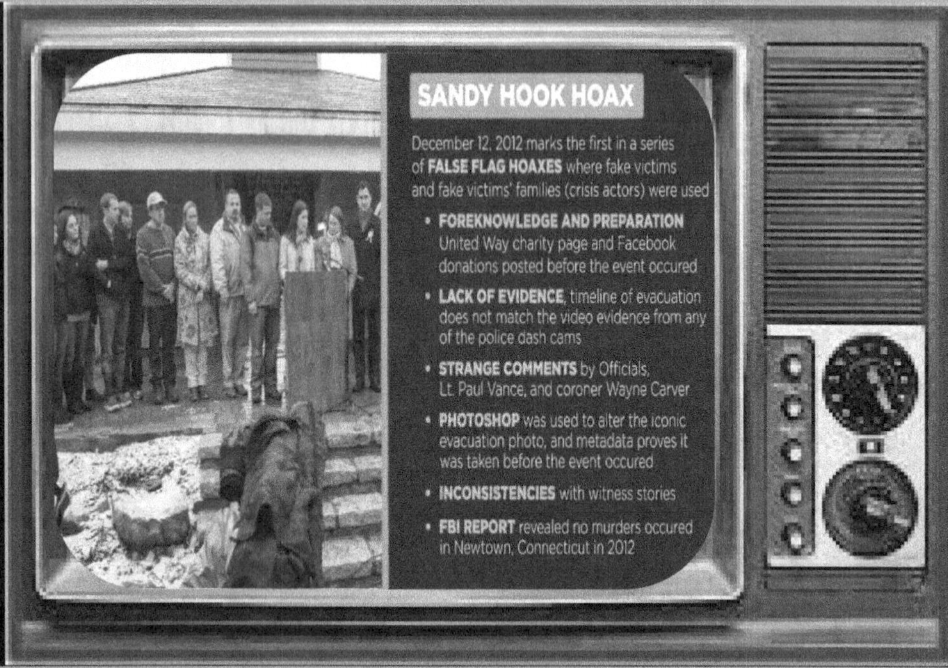

Description: All human-trash featured in this video was produced in
this anti-christ system of indoctrination and deception.
"Unraveling Sandy Hook in 2 3 4 and 5 Dimensions"
LINK: https://www.youtube.com/watch?v=m1yfJDCMU64&t=2753s
"We Need to Talk About Sandy Hook"
LINK: https://www.youtube.com/watch?v=uVII47itn8Q&t=1681s

Shooting Hoaxes

Sandy Hook Line and Sinker New 2017 Documentary

Channel: Rafael Hayes

https://www.youtube.com/watch?v=iUrAN-dDRPo

Description: A very interesting documentary that explores the oddities surrounding the 2012 Sandy Hook school shootings. Video is copyright free so you can share on your .

Shooting Hoaxes

Sandy Hook Visual Anomalies

Channel: William Genske

https://www.youtube.com/watch?v=6ALNl3nUcrQ

Description: No comment

Shooting Hoaxes

Sandy Hook: Actor Gene Rosen Caught Lying Multiple Times And Rehearsing Lines

Channel: thepeople alwayswin

https://www.youtube.com/watch?v=GKPwcPk2x2M

Description: From the recently released documentary, We Need To Talk About Sandy Hook.

Shooting Hoaxes

SOME VERY STRANGE EVIDENCE REVEALED IN TEXAS SHOOTING

Channel: Godrules

https://www.youtube.com/watch?v=-E3nQwDVUXw

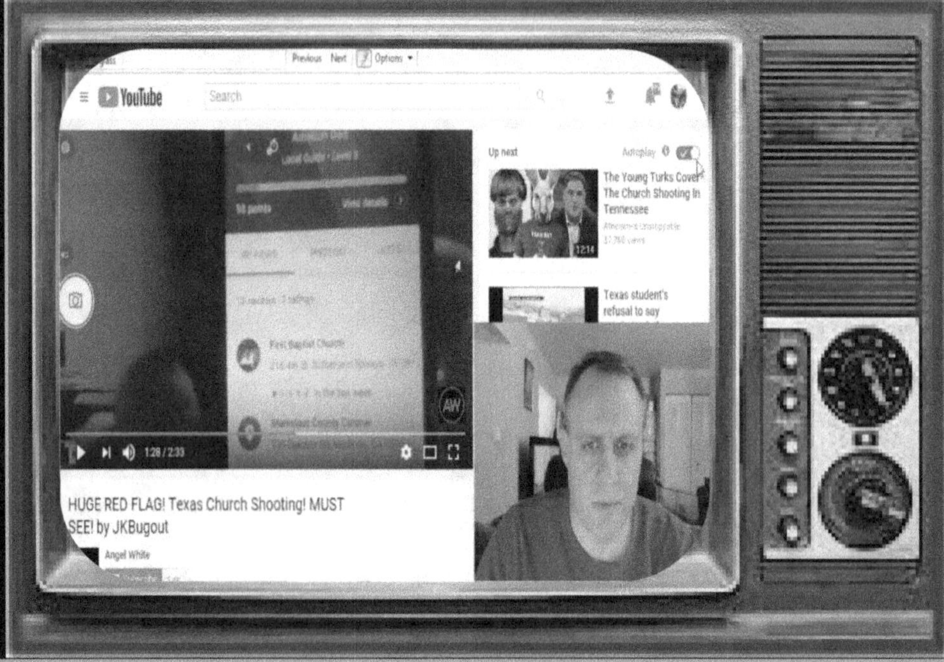

Description: SOME VERY STRANGE EVIDENCE REVEALED IN TEXAS SHOOTING ➡ PROTECT FAMILY DURING A CRISIS - http://www.blackoutusa.org/vsl/index.php?r=5648&r=2522&hop=saledaddy ➡ $0 FOR 10 BOOKS REVEALING ELITE'S PLANS - http://godrules.net/join2c.php   Curiosity Peaked? Watch more great videos and more here on my channel. Also, check out my hosted website for more great topics like this one here!

TOP 201 CONSPIRACY THEORY VIDEOS ON YOUTUBE

Shooting Hoaxes

The FBI and Las Vegas Police are LYING!

Channel: WeAreChange

https://www.youtube.com/watch?v=lU3yoBX8XaE

Description: Jason Bermas exposes two of the major lies being told about the event at that took place in Sin City by both the Las Vegas Police and the FBI.

Visit our MAIN SITE for more breaking news http://wearechange.org/

TOP 201 CONSPIRACY THEORY VIDEOS ON YOUTUBE

Shooting Hoaxes

THE ORLANDO SHOOTING HOAX FULLY EXPOSED

Channel: MAD AS HELL NEWS

https://www.youtube.com/watch?v=NZIjTf4jpsQ

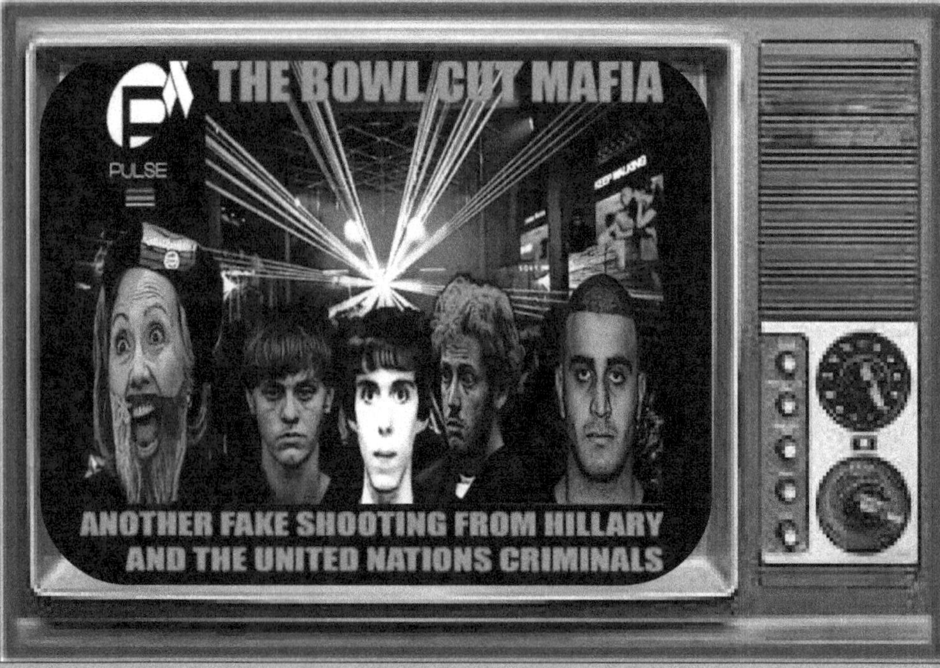

Description: THE ORLANDO SHOOTING WAS A COMPLETE HOAX TO DISARM THE AMERICAN PEOPLE FOR THE UNITED NATIONS GUN BAN THIS VIDEO EXPOSES OBAMA,HILLARY,ERIC HOLDER,MICHAEL BLOOMBERG AND OTHER TREASONOUS SCUM.SPECIAL THANKS TO RED SILVER J,DAHBOO777,BARRY SOETORO AND JEFF C

Shooting Hoaxes

VEGAS CRISIS ACTOR CAUGHT 2 TIMES. FALSE FLAG PROOF AGAIN. SANDYHOOK Podium LAUGHER/VEGAS BYSTANDER

Channel: JONNYY 5

https://www.youtube.com/watch?v=f3ML3c8KQ8I

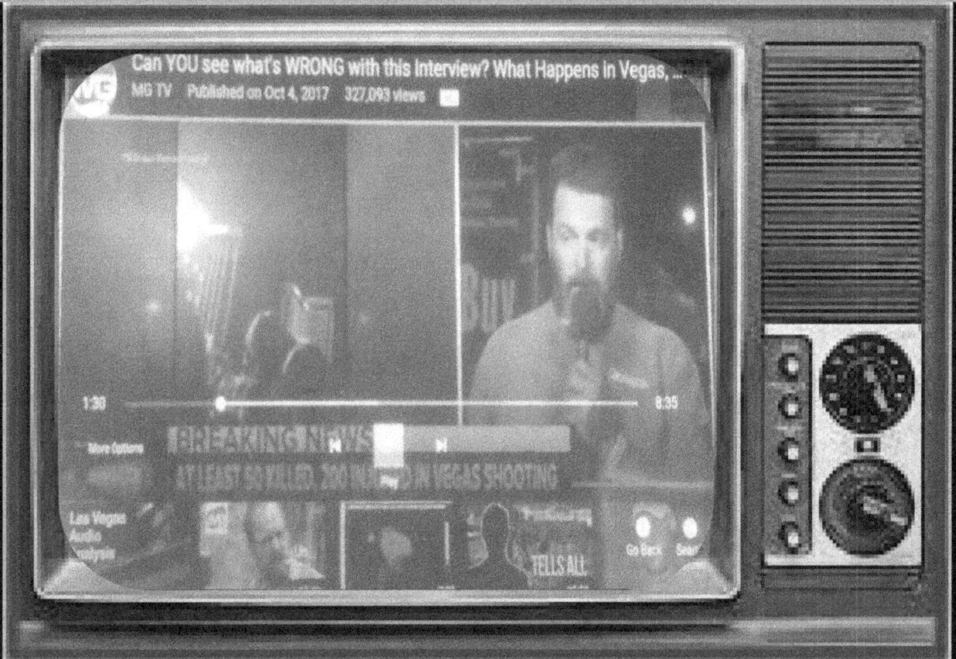

Description: 1st off it seems like everybody comes here to verify Robbie Parker some people say it is some people say it isn't but the ones that definitely do not agree sure do voice their opinion on it I just want to give you my opinion on that I don't care if it is or isn't him I put up this video because I think it's freaking hilarious how this can be presented to the public as truth. who knows I probably had tears in my eyes from laughter when I swear it was him but if you watch the very end...

Shooting Hoaxes

Vegas Massacre - The Search for ANY Evidence of Real Deaths - Part 12 - FINAL

Channel: NowTheTruthTV-15

https://www.youtube.com/watch?v=Hm_nnb6BfM4

Description: Were there ANY real deaths, as a result of the Las Vegas Strip "Massacre"? If so, there would be real bodies (not sand bags) to dispose of, detailed obituaries to notify distant relatives; all would be and should be entered into the record. Is it? Of special interest in this episode: Candice Bowers, who seems to have a studiously average bio, but who appears to actually work for FEMA DHS. Stephen Paddock, the "shooter", who was filmed quite alive and having fun five days AFTER...

Who Killed JFK?

Who Killed JFK?

Dark Legacy: George Bush And The Murder Of John Kennedy

Channel: World Crisis News

https://www.youtube.com/watch?v=-NIJQJUUqR4

Description: A thorough, documented, criminal indictment of George Herbert Walker Bush, establishing beyond a reasonable doubt his guilt as a supervisor in the conspiracy to assassinate John F. Kennedy. You must see it to believe that former president George Herbert Walker Bush was connected to the assassination of JFK. Once you see this documentary though there should be no doubt in your mind that it's true.

Who Killed JFK?

GEORGE H W BUSH ROLE IN THE JFK ASSASSINATION VIDEO

Channel: RICK THORNE

https://www.youtube.com/watch?v=-NlJQJUUqR4

Description: GEORGE H.W. BUSH WAS AT THE TSBD RIGHT AFTER PRESIDENT KENNEDY WAS ASSASSINATED. THIS VIDEO PROVES HIS OCCULT INVOLVEMENT IN THE KENNEDY ASSASSINATION...

Who Killed JFK?

George HW Bush & the JFK Assassination

Channel: JFK Assassination Truth

https://www.youtube.com/watch?v=fRQkDGdHmd0

Description: No comment

Who Killed JFK?

JFK Jr. Told The World What Happened to His Father – But Nobody Was Paying Attention

Channel: Lucid Dreamer

https://www.youtube.com/watch?v=8OcDEkVP1oU&t=2s

Description: I suppose most people think that from the day he saluted his father's casket at just three years old, til the evening his plane went down, he just went about his business, playing the game of life like everyone else.

http://themillenniumreport.com/2017/10/jfk-jr-told-the-world-who-murdered-his-father-but-nobody-was-paying-attention-5/

Who Killed JFK?

JFK to 911 Everything Is A Rich Man's Trick

Channel: Everything Is A Rich Man's Trick

https://www.youtube.com/watch?v=U1Qt6a-vaNM

Description: The who, how & why of the JFK assassination. Taken from an historical perspective starting around world war 1 leading to present day. We hope after watching this video you will know more about what happened in the past and how the world is run today.

Who Killed JFK?

JFK TRUTH - The Mob CIA and the 8 paid ASSASINS

Channel: Porcha Marie Jones

https://www.youtube.com/watch?v=jk_7TCe_Fkk

Description: This is a non monetized, brief encounter to the JFK Murders explained from the film that is over 3 hours long. "JFK 911 A Rich Mans Game" that I shortened to get to THE POINT of the JFK murders truth, and explains why the other conspiracy theories are NOT TRUE. AND THIS IS THE TRUTH YOU HAVE BEEN LOOKING FOR!

Who Killed JFK?

JFK was ASSASSINATED BY THE CIA GEORGE HW BUSH was INVOLVED.avi

Channel: TheRealReginaHicks

https://www.youtube.com/watch?v=PFRv6JxJiwY

Description: No comment

Who Killed JFK?

Photo of George H.W. Bush at Funeral with JFK Proves TREASON

Channel: jeranism

https://www.youtube.com/watch?v=Wap7YX1OeUs

Description: This video is long winded. I have to go through and show how the death of Phil Graham may have not been a suicide and how that research led me to find the photo that proves that George H.W. Bush is guilty of treason and was an accomplice in the murder of John F. Kennedy in 1963. Please understand that my videos are my personal opinions on the world in which we live. You may have similar thoughts or perhaps you disagree. If you disagree and hate me for speaking and...

Who Killed JFK?

The Assassination of JFK Jr

Channel: John Hankey

https://www.youtube.com/watch?v=Vehk03v23y4

Description: No comment

Who Killed JFK?

We know now who killed JFK.

Channel: markwassberg

https://www.youtube.com/watch?v=dN1y6MhfAWk

Description: The truth about JFK how and who killed me. If you believe that Oswald killed him don't be stupid.

Wildfires & Directed Energy Weapons (DEW)

Wildfires & Directed Energy Weapons

5G Microwave Technology And The California Fires
DIRECTED ENERGY WEAPONS # WEDONOTCONSENT

Channel: End Times Productions

https://www.youtube.com/watch?v=yeZN7Z7hRfI

Description: All is not well in California. These fires turned people into ashes, melted steel, and reduced cars into smoldering piles of twisted metal. What really happened here? God bless you all, please stay safe out there people. Thanks for watching. Dear censors, You may think you have the upper hand. However, you are sadly mistaken. YOUR TIME IS RUNNING OUT. We will not sit back and allow this to happen. Go on, keep poking the bear, see what happens. Yours truly -ETP

Wildfires & Directed Energy Weapons

CA "Smart Fires" Likely Started by Airborne Lasers

Channel: aplanetruth.info

https://www.youtube.com/watch?v=LzWyvoGef80

Description: More evidence of highly advanced technology used in CA "Smart Fires" https://www.wired.com/2008/08/will-new-laser/
http://beforeitsnews.com/politics/2016/02/why-are-weaponized-cell-phone-towers-being-constructed-everywhere-2776502.html
Using the excuse that the county/state does not want to use taxpayer funds for debris removal and must require homeowners hand over any debris removal funds from their homeowners insurance is highly...

TOP 201 CONSPIRACY THEORY VIDEOS ON YOUTUBE

Wildfires & Directed Energy Weapons

California Fire Walkthrough Multiple Anomalies

Channel: mental_boost

https://www.youtube.com/watch?v=hGEYU9pKDFk

Description: too many. what is up with that dirt mound smoldering for days? why doesn't anyone just get a shovel and start investigating this?

Wildfires & Directed Energy Weapons

California Fires: Terracotta Roof Anomaly: Microwave Assisted Combustion Synthesis

Channel: inTruthbyGrace

https://www.youtube.com/watch?v=_1g_GbZO3pE&t=1s

Description: Most of the SoCal fire "anomalies" are easily explained by the natural science of microwave-assisted combustion synthesis.... microwave assisted combustion is NOT a natural occurrence _but_ the observations of what happens when electric fields of material are manipulated, is quite predictable and sadly, this seems to be exactly what is being documented in these videos of the cal fire.

Wildfires & Directed Energy Weapons

Directed Energy Weapons Are Being Used To Cause Strange Wildfires

Channel: Anon Ehmus

https://www.youtube.com/watch?v=faAuK5T9Tyg

Description: Related Blog Article:
https://redpillinfowar.com/2017/10/17/directed-energy-weapons-are-being-used-to-cause-strange-wildfires/
I don't usually jump to conclusions when it comes to the current event of today and those items presented to me for consideration of the content within. When I first heard anything of interest to my palate on these fires, I was presented with a video showing drone footage of...

Wildfires & Directed Energy Weapons

FOX NEWS ADMITS GOVERNMENT USING LASERS (DEW) BEFORE CA FIRES

Channel: Futureman19

https://www.youtube.com/watch?v=-cT-E-zXLlI

Description: No Longer a Conspiracy Theory but Conspiracy FACT: On September 28, 2017, about 10 days before the Northern California Fires in Wine Country began, Fox News ADMITS to the government having Laser Technology or Directed Energy Weapons (DEW). ATHENA, (Advanced Test High Energy Asset), is one of the most exciting of these new American laser weapons.

Wildfires & Directed Energy Weapons

LAZERS CAUGHT STARTING FIRES?!
TREE BURNS FROM INSIDE OUT?!

Channel: Joanne Steen

https://www.youtube.com/watch?v=MvQ599ZPAtw

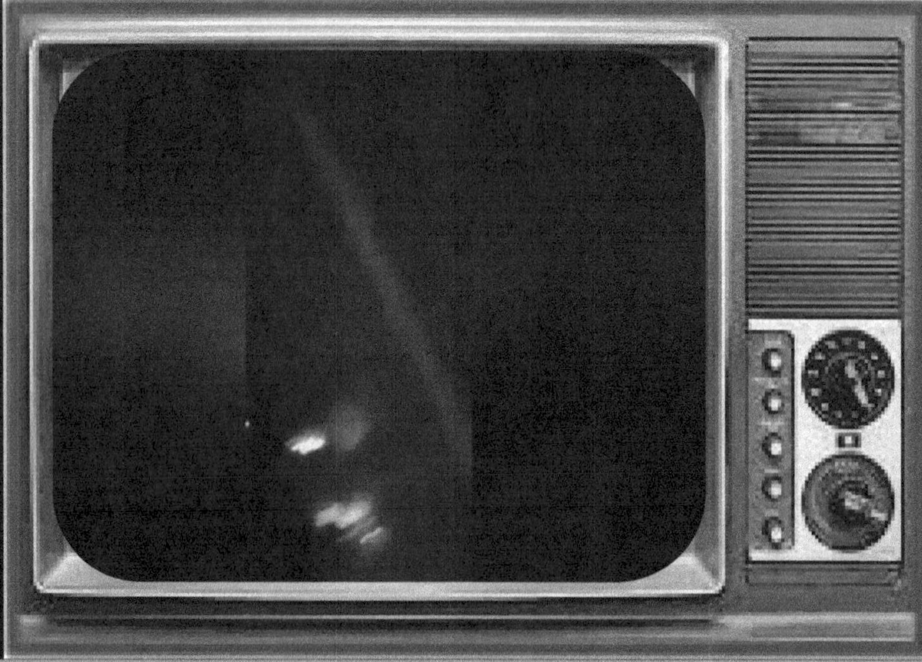

Description: https://www.youtube.com/watch?v=ykiXHSvZuP8
LINK TO THATS IMPOSSIBLE CHANNE;L
https://www.youtube.com/watch?v=KAaiSjznt68
LINK TO LEAK PROJECT
https://www.facebook.com/profile.php?id=100004809254595

Wildfires & Directed Energy Weapons

Portugal Madeira Wildfire DIRECTED ENERGY WEAPON

Channel: Terrarium Firma

https://www.youtube.com/watch?v=L8zvJYPA9mY

Description: No comment

Wildfires & Directed Energy Weapons

Proof California Fires Caused by High Tech Weapons!

Channel: Emily Windsor-Cragg

https://www.youtube.com/watch?v=vu3zcKp0NJI&t=18s

Description: Brought here from by the Truth Warriors, as a public service.

Wildfires & Directed Energy Weapons

Proof of Weather Modification
NASA, HAARP & Chemtrail Technology ▶

Channel: ODD Reality

https://www.youtube.com/watch?v=wJBBlntDtEU

Description: Weather hasn't been natural since the mid 1900's or maybe even earlier and NASA has it's name written all over it. Of course, HAARP and HAARP-like facilities as well as chemtrails play their role. Weather modification programs have been active for decades and still people choose to ignore them and act they are only "conspiracy theories". In this video I am breaking down older technolgies, but there are new ones like NEXRAD and SBX-1.

Wildfires & Directed Energy Weapons

Visible Proof Lasers Used in 911 Cal Fires

Channel: aplaintruth.info

https://www.youtube.com/watch?v=AS4FUtpZ6vA

Description: Three separate recordings and dozens of comments by those who w
here that saw blue lights in the sky the night of the 9.11 CA Fires.
https://www.youtube.com/watch?v=KbLljrGV5gI
https://www.youtube.com/watch?v=yB55k8HMuA8&t=166s

Wildfires & Directed Energy Weapons

Weekend Geo Engineering In Sydney

Channel: Nate Max TV

https://www.youtube.com/watch?v=dh1ly84BKeA

Description: Hey people another eye witness account of some Geo-Engineering programs happening around Sydney and Australia

Wildfires & Directed Energy Weapons

Wildfire 2017 California-Drone footage-KMart Burned -Trees Untouched!!!!Officials Asked about DEW

Channel: Serbian Conspiracy

https://www.youtube.com/watch?v=vrgUpkAcOH4

Description: Drone footage over Santa Rosa and North California shows that only houses and cars burned, while Trees next to is not.